HEALING THE HURT
IN YOUR MARRIAGE

HEALING

THE
HURT
IN

YOUR
MARRIAGE

DR. GARY & BARBARA ROSBERG

TYNDALE HOUSE PUBLISHERS, INC.
WHEATON, ILLINOIS

Visit Tyndale's exciting Web site at www.tyndale.com

Healing the Hurt in Your Marriage

This book is a marriage-focused adaptation of *Dr. Rosberg's Do-It-Yourself Relationship Mender* by Gary Rosberg, a Focus on the Family book published by Tyndale House Publishers, ISBN 1-56179-760-X, Wheaton, Illinois 60189,© 1992, 1995. This book was originally published under the title *Choosing to Love Again: Restoring Broken Relationships,* a Focus on the Family book distributed by Word Books, ISBN 1-56179-0958, Dallas, Texas, © 1992.

Some of the names and details in the illustrations used in this book have been changed to protect the privacy of the people who shared their stories with us.

Designed by Alyssa Force

Edited by Lynn Vanderzalm

A Focus on the Family book published by Tyndale House Publishers, Inc., Wheaton, Illinois 60189

ISBN 1-58997-104-3

Printed in the United States of America

09   08   07   06   05   04
8   7   6   5   4   3   2   1

God has called us to commit our ministry to divorce-proofing
America's marriages, and we aren't doing it alone. We dedicate
this book to Ron Beers and our publishing team at Tyndale House,
Greg Anderson and our radio team at Salem Radio Network,
and our ministry team at America's Family Coaches.
Together, we are encouraging, equipping,
and coaching America's families.

CONTENTS

Acknowledgments

As we have committed our ministry and lives to divorce-proofing America's marriages, we have surrounded ourselves with some of the most gifted and talented men and women in America. We want to acknowledge these tremendous friends for committing this season of their lives to a campaign to encourage both healthy families and hurting families.

Ron Beers and the Beers Group at Tyndale House Publishers have equipped us to bring you this book and each of the books we publish. We have more than a publishing relationship with Tyndale House. It is a partnership and friendship. Thank you to Ken Petersen, Jon Farrar, Lynn Vanderzalm, MaryLynn Layman, Mary Keeley, Brian Ondracek, Tammy Faxel, Carol Traver, Linda Taylor, Jim Baird, and the entire publishing team. Special thanks to Ed Stewart, who has helped us bring this manuscript to life. Ron, you have surrounded yourself with the finest publishing group in Christian publishing. Thank you for stewarding your team to help us equip America with this message. Your friendship and commitment have changed our lives.

Greg Anderson and the Salem Radio Network have propelled this published message to the radio airwaves. Your commitment to us and our message is changing marriages and families forever. We can't thank you enough for equipping us to bring our message to marriages and families across America each day. We give special thanks to Charles Mefferd.

Our board and ministry team at America's Family Coaches is the most extraordinary group we have ever met. We are not only proud of you and love your hearts, but we are amazed at your giftedness, diligence, and enthusiasm for ministering to families. As we sharpen our message and watch God expand our borders, you are the gracious friends that make it all happen.

Focus on the Family believed in the message of this book as it was published several years ago in a different form and with different titles. We thank Focus on the Family for their partnership in this book.

To our pastor, Quintin Stieff, of Valley Evangelical Free Church in West Des Moines, Iowa, thank you for shepherding our family so well. Your commitment to us, our message, and our family is a gift that encourages us daily. We love you, Pastor.

And finally, to our precious family. What a joy to be Mom and Dad to Sarah and Scott, and Missy and Cooper. You four are loved beyond your wildest imagination. Mason and Kaden, our grandsons, you are our legacy. Thank you to all of you, for bringing joy, laughter, and memories to your mom and dad. You are a blast!

Gary and Barbara Rosberg

INTRODUCING THE DIVORCE-PROOFING AMERICA'S MARRIAGES CAMPAIGN

$\mathcal{D}$ear friend,

The book in your hands is a vital part of a campaign to Divorce-Proof America's Marriages. Couples across this nation—from Boston to Los Angeles, from Miami to Seattle—are joining together to divorce-proof their marriages. They are taking a stand *for* healthy, growing, lifetime marriages and *against* the looming threat of divorce.

Why now?

If we don't do it *now,* then when?

If we don't start *here*—with our family and yours—then where?

If we don't do it *together,* who will?

We believe that if we fail to address divorce now, the next generation of marriages will be lost. We must catch the vision for divorce-proofed marriages and push back the threat of divorce as far as our influence can reach. We want to join you not only in proactively protecting your own marriage but in helping divorce-proof the marriage of every couple you know.

As we go to battle together for the cause of the Christian home, we will pay a price. We have a powerful enemy in this endeavor. The apostle Peter warns, "Be careful! Watch out for attacks from the Devil, your great enemy. He prowls around like a roaring lion, looking for some victim to devour" (1 Peter 5:8).

You and your marriage are the devil's intended victims. Since a divorce-proof marriage is high on God's priority list, you can know that such marriages are also at the top of the enemy's hit list. Satan would like nothing better than to discourage you, debilitate your marriage, and add another crippled or broken family to his ledger. That is why we are asserting that your marriage and family *are* your ministry.

Let us proclaim together loudly and clearly: Divorce will stop—and stop *now*. Starting in our home and in yours, let's draw a line in the sand and tell anyone with ears to hear, "As for me and my family, we will serve the Lord" (Joshua 24:15). Let's agree to pull out all the stops in order to build biblical homes—for the sake of our marriages, for the sake of the next generation, and for the cause of Jesus Christ.

But it doesn't stop there. If you—as a couple, a pastor, a small-group leader, adult Sunday school teacher—share these principles with other couples and families you care about, you will become part of God's work to change the face of marriage in our country. (For additional resources as well as ideas about how to start a small group in your community, please see the appendix).

How does *Healing the Hurt in Your Marriage* fit into the campaign? We believe that many marriages suffer from unresolved conflict that can cause hurt and anger. If we do not learn to close the loop on our conflicts, our marriages will be at risk for sliding toward disconnection, discord, and possibly emotional divorce. Forgiving love—the kind of love that faces the inevitable conflicts and heals wounds—is a critical part of divorce-proofing any marriage. This book will help you develop and practice forgiving love, one of the six different kinds of love outlined in our campaign book, *Divorce-Proof Your Marriage*.

We hope you catch the vision for divorce-proofing your marriage—and the marriages of people you know. It's a campaign worth investing in!

Your friends,
Gary and Barb Rosberg

Have You Ever Been Hurt?

Have you ever been hurt in your marriage relationship? Like most married couples, the Thompsons have. Jan and Zach look great on the outside. Thirteen years of marriage, good jobs, a couple of kids, leadership positions in their church, a house in the suburbs, a ski boat—they have it all. But behind closed doors there is conflict, especially over Zach's mom. Ever since Zach's dad died, his mother has tried to run his life. Much to Jan's dismay, Zach does whatever his mom wants him to do, and it is squeezing the life out of Jan. She calls it unhealthy control and manipulation. He calls it honoring his mother. Jan secretly wonders how long she can endure being the "other woman" in her husband's life.

The ongoing argument between Jan and Zach remains unresolved. They are gridlocked on the issue, yet on either side of this wall of defensiveness are two deeply loving people who long for understanding, care, and validation from each other. Both have a high need for support, but instead of showing their soft side to each other, they stand back to back with hardened hearts.

Angry, defensive, and critical words have piled up into a mountain between them, and the words "I'm sorry" and "I forgive you" have disappeared from their vocabulary. Neither of them likes what is happening, but when they hurt each other, all they know to do is retaliate, bringing more hurt. If they don't find help soon, the Thompsons may eventually see their names in the newspaper's public notices under the heading Divorces.

Have you ever been hurt in your marriage relationship? Gideon has. It was the biggest night of his career, his company's annual awards banquet. Gideon's hard work had finally paid off, and he was recognized as employee of the year. He was the star of the banquet. And along with the acclaim and applause came a $1,000 bonus. It was a night to remember—except for one huge disappointment: Keisha didn't attend the banquet with him.

Three hours before they were to leave for the banquet, Gideon's wife of six years announced that she was spending the evening with her sister. Gideon was blindsided by her statement, having assumed that Keisha was as excited about his award as he was. "That's your world, honey," she had said. "I don't know those people, so the evening would be very boring for me. You go and have a good time." Driving home after the festivities, Gideon found himself wondering if he made a mistake by marrying Keisha. Not knowing how to connect with his wife, he feels like shutting down and not trying anymore.

Have you ever been hurt in your marriage relationship? Laura has. When she met Dave at a singles' Bible study, she knew he was the man she had been waiting for. God had certainly kept her from committing to any other man so he could save her for Dave. He asked her out the night they met and they fell deeply in love. They were married a year later.

Their first year of marriage was like a fairy tale. Dave would send Laura little notes and call her unexpectedly during the day just to say, "Hi, honey, I love you." He brought her flowers and gifts. He took her on dates. Laura's church friends were so happy for her.

Then Dave's career suddenly took off, and along with the promotions came the big money. It was great until Laura noticed that

Dave is too busy working to send notes and to call. Now he has to work many evenings, which means they practically never go out. And when Dave does come home early, he doesn't want to talk much. Exhausted, he just eats dinner and falls asleep in front of the TV. Laura cries herself to sleep many nights because she feels Dave slipping away from her. His career has become his mistress, and Laura doesn't know how to win him back.

Have you ever been hurt in your marriage relationship? JoAnne has. Her husband, Randy, took the checkbook away from her. "I think you're spending too much," Randy said when JoAnne asked if he had seen the checkbook. "So I'm going to pay the bills from now on. You can have some spending money, but if you need to buy groceries or something else for the house, I'll write the check for you."

At first JoAnne thought it was a joke—and a poor one at that. But Randy is serious. JoAnne, who managed her own finances as a single woman, argues the point. But Randy won't relent, convinced that he is better suited to take care of their money. JoAnne feels humiliated by his decision, but she refuses to allow Randy the satisfaction of knowing how badly she feels. She will get even somehow.

Have you ever been hurt in your marriage relationship? Jack has. He and Lynda have been married fourteen years. Jack has worked hard to provide a nice home for her and their three kids. He knows Lynda hates his graveyard shift, and he doesn't like it either. Leaving home at 8:00 P.M. really messes up his time with the kids. And it limits his intimate moments with his wife.

But Jack *has* to work graveyard. He and Lynda decided early on that Lynda would stay home with the kids. So Jack's graveyard bonus pays for things they can't otherwise afford, including braces, clarinet lessons, and church camp for the kids. Jack hopes his next promotion will allow him to switch back to working days.

Then one night around midnight, Jack cut his hand on the job, and his supervisor told him to go home. Instead of calling to wake up Lynda and the kids, Jack drove himself to the emergency room for stitches and then headed home. He walked in on Lynda and a guy from his Bible study group locked in a passionate embrace on the sofa. Jack was devastated, and Lynda was mortified. They still love each other, but they don't know how to deal with what has happened between them.

MARITAL BREAKDOWNS

Have you ever been hurt by your spouse? Sure you have. Have you ever been the cause of pain in your partner's life? Absolutely. In every marriage relationship, the husband and wife have both been the offended and the offender, the cause and the recipient of marital pain. There are no exceptions, including Barb and me, who have committed our lives to strengthening and divorce-proofing marriages across the country.

We talk with people like Jan, Zach, Gideon, Laura, JoAnne, Jack—and you—practically every day. They phone-in during our daily nationally syndicated radio program, *America's Family Coaches . . . Live!* They come up to us between sessions at the many marriage conferences we host each year around the country. They call our office, and sometimes they pull us aside at church, in the mall, at a restaurant—wherever. These husbands, wives, and couples share stories of struggle, conflict, and hurt in their marriages. Some of the problems are very serious, even marriage-threatening. Most are relatively minor and common. But the hurt still hurts, and they come to us for help and healing.

Why do we hurt each other as husband and wife? Why do two people who have committed to love each other for a lifetime sometimes forget each other, ignore each other, or turn on each other? Because every marriage is made up of two imperfect people who are sometimes thoughtless, insensitive, unkind, or downright selfish. And two imperfect people sharing the same space are bound to get into disagreements. We all get into these marital "fender benders" now and then, no matter how much we may wish to avoid them and how sad we feel when they happen.

It's kind of like driving on our crowded streets and freeways. None of us ever intends to have an accident, but it happens sometimes. Even if you drive defensively and have a perfect record, some of the people around you don't. Someone follows too closely, tries to race through on a yellow light, forgets to check the mirror before changing lanes, or backs out of a parking space without looking. A momentary lapse of driver alertness and—*crunch!* You have a fender bender to deal with—or worse.

Every marriage has its share of relational misunderstandings and mistakes, clashes and cold shoulders, sharp words and shouting matches that result in pain. And sometimes it's more like a head-on collision causing major damage—such as betrayal, unfaithfulness, or abuse. It doesn't matter how deeply you and your spouse love each other, conflict and hurt at some level are inevitable. It's not a question of *if,* only *when.*

So what do you do when it happens? How do you respond when a conflict brings hurt to you, your spouse, or both of you? Many couples, like the examples opening this chapter, don't know what to do. So they do nothing and inevitably drift apart. Diane Sollee, founder and director of the Coalition for Marriage, Family, and Couples Education, states, "The number one predictor of divorce is the habitual avoidance of conflict."[1]

Most marriage surveys reveal that resolving conflict and hurt is right up there with communication as the biggest problem facing couples. Our own experience at America's Family Coaches bears this out. We know what to do when we tangle bumpers with another driver. We exchange names and insurance information, we get estimates and repairs from the body shop, and soon we're back on the road again. Yet so many of us today are clueless about how to resolve marital breakdowns.

Why? Because no one taught us how to do it. Healthy conflict resolution was not modeled in many of our homes as we grew up. However, conflict, alienation, and divorce were modeled. Research reflects that "seventy percent of all persons in our society have been impacted by divorce—either the divorce of their parents or their own."[2] If we don't find the answers at home, where will we find them? We sure don't see programs about healthy conflict resolution on prime-time TV. And often we don't even learn how to resolve marital conflict in church. So rather than heal our hurts and move on with life, we allow our problems to pile up, mistakenly thinking—or secretly wishing—that time really does heal all wounds. It doesn't. Instead, over time, unresolved conflicts and unhealed hurts harden our hearts and drive a wedge between us as husbands and wives.

And the pain doesn't stop there. When we bury our conflicts instead of facing them, when we stuff our pain instead of dealing with it, a process is set in motion. You may think you get rid of conflict by burying it, but you are burying it alive and it will continue to haunt you. Avoidance will eventually lead you toward a place you don't want to go: emotional divorce. You may never physically separate or file for legal divorce for a number of reasons such as appearances, the children, or religious convictions. But the distance between you will continue to widen to a relational disconnect and an emotional divorce. You will feel stuck and unhappy living in the same house and sharing the same name. The marriage dream you once shared will die a slow and painful death. All that's missing is publicly filing the paperwork in the county courthouse.

When your spouse talks about the importance of your marriage, listen to him or her. Spouses who see their troubled marriage as viable will usually talk about the problems and suggest that measures be taken to improve it. When they stop talking, beware; it may mean they have stopped trying. If this pattern of emotional withdrawal continues for six months or more, this spouse may end up walking away physically.

THE PATH OF FORGIVING LOVE

Barb and I don't want to be anywhere near that road to emotional divorce, and we don't want you there either. In order to keep moving in the direction of your marriage dream and far away from disconnect and divorce, three things need to happen.

First, you need to come to grips with the reality that you and your spouse cause each other pain from time to time. It may not be intentional, and you may not even be aware of when it's happening. But it happens in the day-to-day course of your life together through what you say or fail to say and through what you do or fail to do. Admit that both of you are responsible. You are both victims and culprits in the marital pain you experience. Face it: It takes *two* to tango, and it takes *two* to tangle!

Second, you need to know what to do when the inevitable conflicts and pain occur in your marriage. Conflicts must be resolved. Offenses must be confessed and forgiven. Hurts must be healed. The Bible has a plan for working through marital door dings, fender benders, and head-on collisions. You both need to internalize that plan until it becomes second nature.

Third, you need to put God's plan into practice when conflict and hurt happen in your marriage. Knowing what to do isn't enough. Warm feelings and a positive attitude about your spouse are insufficient. Good intentions won't cut it. Even prayer won't accomplish everything, though it is the essential starting place. Let us teach you a biblical plan so that, when the next conflict rears its ugly head, you will know how to handle it by doing the right thing.

As Jesus said to his disciples, "Now that you know these things, you will be blessed if you do them" (John 13:17, NIV).

This book will help you take all three steps. Barb and I will coach you in the skills that will help you build what we call *forgiving love* into your marriage relationship. You will learn how to resolve your conflicts—great and small—before they accumulate and grow into a wall between you. We will guide you through a process that will help you heal emotional wounds before the gangrene of distance and disconnect poisons your marriage. As forgiving love becomes a daily expression in your life together, you will take major steps toward divorce-proofing your marriage.

To get started, Barb is going to give you a brief overview of where we are headed.

A LOOK AT THE LOOP

Before we founded the nationwide ministry of America's Family Coaches, Gary counseled families in private practice. During those years he listened to people pour out the pain of their marriage and family relationships every hour of the workday all week long. This is when God gave him insight to draw up a plan to help couples visualize where they were in their marital breakdown, determine how they got there, and experience biblical principles for forgiving love. As he listened to hundreds of hurting people pour out their marital pain, Gary noticed a common thread of events woven through virtually every sad story. As he analyzed this sequence, he developed a concept that has helped heal and revitalize countless marriages. It's the same concept we use in our ministry across the country today and the concept we will share with you in the chapters ahead. We refer to it as "The Loop." Here's how it works. (See the diagram in figure 1.)

The Open Loop of Conflict. Marital conflict begins with an offense of some kind. Your spouse says or does something harmful to you, whether intentionally or unintentionally. The offense provokes an emotional reaction: You are hurt and then angered. We picture this as an open loop of conflict in your relationship. At this point, your spouse may not even be aware that something is wrong.

Instead of addressing the offense and resolving the conflict, many offended spouses respond in ways that only make things worse. You may strike back verbally or in your actions, venting your anger on your spouse. You may bury your anger and let it simmer, hoping to keep the peace until the rift blows over. Or you may just give up and let your spouse have his or her way. In time the issue dies down, and the two of you go on with life. But the painful loop is still open.

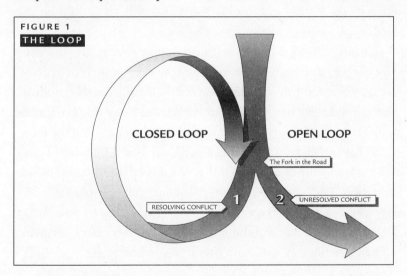

FIGURE 1
THE LOOP

CLOSED LOOP   OPEN LOOP

The Fork in the Road

RESOLVING CONFLICT   1   2   UNRESOLVED CONFLICT

Many couples live with dozens of open loops in their marriages. Gary and I have heard their heartbreaking stories. Unresolved conflicts and unhealed hurts pile up on each other. Smoldering anger grows into bitterness, resentment, apathy, or even hatred. And with each additional conflict, husband and wife drift further from each other and closer to emotional divorce. In part 1 of this book, we will explore in detail the pain and pitfalls of ignoring the open loops of conflict in your marriage.

The Fork in the Road. Whenever an offense opens a loop in your relationship, you have a choice. You can decide to do what is needed to close the loop, or you can do nothing and suffer the painful consequences. Sounds like a no-brainer decision, doesn't it? Yet our experience over the years has convinced us that husbands and wives have difficulty choosing to heal their hurts. In part 2, we will look more closely at this important choice and identify some common hindrances to it.

The Closed Loop of Healing. The Bible provides clear instructions for resolving conflict and healing hurts. Once you make the choice to exercise forgiving love in your marriage, God will empower you for the task by his Spirit and will set in motion the healing process.

Closing the loop begins with preparing your heart, diffusing your anger, and communicating your concerns to your spouse. Next, you need to confront your conflicts, forgive your spouse, and rebuild your trust as husband and wife. In part 3, Gary and I will coach you through these important steps for closing the loop.

What we share with you is a biblically based plan for healing the hurts in your marriage. God's Word is full of instruction, admonition, and encouragement about our relationships at every level, including marriage. Gary is going to relate to you one of Jesus' parables that is foundational to the process of forgiving love in marriage as well as in other relationships.

A Word Picture of Healing

You are probably familiar with the story of the Prodigal Son, found in Luke 15:11-24. Jesus' parable is a timeless illustration and example of opening and closing the loop: conflict, hurt, resolution, healing. In his story, the Master offers us both hope and help for restoring broken relationships.

The Open Loop of Conflict. The story begins with the younger of
two sons demanding that his father hand over his share of the family
estate. What a slap in the face! In New Testament times, the greatest offense a son could commit was to prematurely ask for his inheritance. It would be like your teenaged son or daughter demanding,
"I want my inheritance now because you are dead to me."

Amazingly, the father met the young man's demand by fork-
ing over his inheritance. Perhaps the dad knew that the head-
strong lad was beyond his control. Then again, maybe this wise
and loving dad knew that by releasing the boy's inheritance, he
might open a door for God to do something in his son's hard
heart, ultimately leading father and son to a restored relationship.

As if the son hadn't hurt his father enough the text says, "A few
days later this younger son packed all his belongings and took a
trip to a distant land, and there he wasted all his money on wild
living" (Luke 15:13). Imagine how the father felt when the boy
thumbed his nose at him and the family farm and walked away.
Also, imagine the reaction of the other dads in the community: "If
my boy pulled a stunt like that, I would tell him, 'No way, get
back to the fields!'"; "My kid would never make it, and when he
failed, I would never let him return." But this dad was different.

The parable doesn't tell us how long it took the party animal to
run through his cash. It could have been only a few weeks, or it
could have been months. But then reality set in. He was broke and
far from home—and his dad wasn't there to bail him out. At that
point the son could have returned home, but he was probably too
proud. The story continues, "About the time his money ran out, a
great famine swept over the land, and he began to starve. He per-
suaded a local farmer to hire him to feed his pigs. The boy became
so hungry that even the pods he was feeding the pigs looked good
to him. But no one gave him anything" (Luke 15:14-16).

Can you imagine this scene? This hard-hearted boy, who had it
all back home, was probably hungry for the first time in his life. I

believe God used the young man's hunger for food to plant the idea in his head that his greater hunger was for a restored relationship with his father. Yet God had to do something in the boy's heart before he could return home.

In the meantime, how was the father holding up in the midst of the conflict? He must have missed the boy terribly. He must have grieved his son's rejection of everything he stood for: solid work ethic, responsible living, righteous conduct. And yet he kept his eye on the road in hopes that his son would return to him someday. I can just see the father walking from the house out to the road wondering, *Will today be the day my beloved son comes home?*

The Fork in the Road. Finally the young man reached the end of his rope. He realized he had made a big mistake. He had not only ruined his own life; he had also greatly offended his father. He stood at a fork in the road. It was time to make a choice. Would he leave the loop open forever—rationalizing his behavior, blaming others, wallowing in self-pity and relentless guilt? Or would he choose to close the loop and restore his relationship with his father?

Back to the narrative. "When he finally came to his senses, he said to himself, 'At home even the hired men have food enough to spare, and here I am, dying of hunger! I will go home to my father and say, "Father, I have sinned against both heaven and you, and I am no longer worthy of being called your son. Please take me on as a hired man"'" (Luke 15:17-19). The lad knew he must humble himself and confess his sin in order to make things right.

But how would the prodigal's father respond? Would his father reject him? That's what he deserved. That's what he had done to his father. Yet the boy knew that he must go home. Pride had been replaced by a broken heart. Once holding fast to a demanding, self-centered outlook on life, the prodigal now desired to restore a broken relationship. So he turned his steps toward home.

I can't help but think that the prayers of a loving father had encouraged the prodigal to this critical realization.

The Closed Loop of Healing. Then something wonderful happened in the parable:

> So he returned home to his father. And while he was still a long distance away, his father saw him coming. Filled with love and compassion, he ran to his son, embraced him, and kissed him. His son said to him, "Father, I have sinned against both heaven and you, and I am no longer worthy of being called your son."
>
> But his father said to the servants, "Quick! Bring the finest robe in the house and put it on him. Get a ring for his finger, and sandals for his feet. And kill the calf we have been fattening in the pen. We must celebrate with a feast, for this son of mine was dead and has now returned to life. He was lost, but now he is found." So the party began. (Luke 15:20-24)

I get goose bumps realizing that the father in the story was even more eager to close the loop than his wayward son was. The father saw his boy coming from a long way off. But he didn't stand on the porch waiting for him. He took off running to meet him. Throwing his arms around his repentant son, the father granted him complete forgiveness and restored him to fellowship.

What a scene! Can you see the tears of joy? Can you hear the music of celebration in the background? Can you feel the peace of a broken relationship made whole? Barb and I love this parable and how it pictures God's heart for healing hurts.

And if you like this happy ending, imagine what's in store for you and your spouse as you begin to exercise forgiving love in your marriage. Husbands and wives are even closer than fathers and sons. The pain of the open loop is even greater in marriage, and the joy and peace of healing is even sweeter. You can reenact the final scene of this parable over and over in your own experience as you learn to close the loop on conflict and hurt. Let us show you how in the pages ahead.

PART I

THE OPEN LOOP
OF CONFLICT

Blindsided by an Offense

We had the most wonderful marriage of anyone I know, Gary. We raised three fantastic children, and now we have a new grandchild who is the light of our lives. Then, three weeks ago, Nancy walked away and my world fell apart."

The man sitting in my office was highly respected in our community for his Christian character, leadership, and influence. Dean was at the top of his game in every area. He had a successful career. He was a leader and teacher in the men's ministry at his church. And he assumed that his marriage was secure. Nancy's sudden departure had blindsided Dean. The dark circles under his eyes revealed how painful the past three weeks had been for him. He had been knocked down and was nearly out.

Dean continued, "Nancy is the last woman in the world I would expect to do this. She is such a great mother. Everyone loves her. I know I have been busy. I know I haven't responded to her as I should. The spark may have been dimmed a little in our relationship, but I never thought she would leave me. All marriages go through times of disconnect, don't they? I didn't think ours was such a big deal."

"Is there another man?" I asked.

Dean nodded forlornly. "A customer she met at work. With the kids gone and my career flying high, Nancy got a part-time job, something to get her out of the empty nest. This guy kept coming into the shop. She never told me about him, but she began to change. She wore more perfume, bought new clothes, and there was a sparkle in her I hadn't seen in years. Now I know why. Nancy was lit up because of another man's affection."

"How did you find out about this man?" I asked.

"I was rummaging through the cupboard of our laundry room looking for the key to our shed," Dean said. "I found a greeting card tucked behind some stuff, kind of hidden. It looked like a card I could have given Nancy a few years back—you know, mushy and romantic. But it wasn't from me; it was from somebody named Tim. I couldn't believe what I read. It was as if this guy knew every intimate part of my wife that I knew—and more!"

"What did you do?"

"I walked into the family room where Nancy was sorting through the mail. I dropped the card on the top of the pile in front of her. She looked at it and then slowly looked up at me. She said she never meant to hurt me, but she didn't know me anymore.

"I said, 'Tell me this is a joke or just a way to get my attention. Tell me this isn't real.' She said, 'It's real. I'm sorry you are hurt, but I'm not sorry you found out. I'll pack. I already have an apartment.' There were tears in her eyes.

"Gary, I have heard you talk about the walk-away wife, but I never thought I would be sitting in your office telling you that Nancy is a walk-away wife. She stopped talking when I stopped listening. I rationalized my preoccupation with work was building our retirement. But I realize now that I was so full of myself that I couldn't hear what she was trying to tell me about her needs—until it was too late."

"What did you do when Nancy told you she would pack and move out?"

"It was strange. Part of me wanted to reach out to her. That's my job as a husband—you know, what the Bible says about comforting each other. Another part of me wanted to wring her neck. I have never felt that kind of confusion in my life. I just started to cry. I haven't done that in years. We stood there for several minutes looking at each other and crying.

"Nancy said she wanted to tell me everything, but she was afraid. Hearing her say 'I have an apartment' blew me away. I never imagined I would hear those words come out of her mouth."

Barb and I hear about walk-away wives frequently on our daily radio program. When there is serious conflict in a marriage, it is usually the wife who leaves. Author and marriage expert Michele Weiner-Davis reports, "Approximately two-thirds of the divorces in our country are filed by women."[1]

THE INEVITABILITY OF MARITAL OFFENSES

Notice Dean's last statement: "I never imagined I would hear those words come out of her mouth." Barb and I can't calculate the number of times we have heard a wounded husband or wife say something like that. Describing the hurt they have suffered in their marriages, they exclaim:

* "I can't believe he would do something so cruel."
* "I knew she was unhappy, but I never expected this!"
* "Why would he lie to me—his own wife? It's unthinkable."
* "What did I do to deserve such treatment?"
* "How did we allow our marriage to get to such a low point?"

Dean's heartbreaking experience reminds us that a marriage relationship, including ours and yours, is not all sweetness and light. We offend each other. (See the diagram in figure 2.) Offenses happen, and every one of them opens a painful loop in the relationship. But when offenses happen, they often surprise us because we just don't expect marriage to be a place of hurt. Dean certainly didn't expect the pain he was experiencing. We will tell you more of Dean and Nancy's story later.

Most people launch into matrimony with an idealistic view of marital harmony. Have you ever talked to engaged couples? Have you seen that glazed-over gleam in their eyes? Have you heard them say about each other, "I'm marrying a perfect gentleman" or "My wife-to-be is my dream come true"? They are so overcome with feelings of love and visions of a fairy-tale marriage that they are numb to the inevitability of conflicts and offenses. That's fairly typical of most couples, and it's probably how you and your spouse began your marital journey.

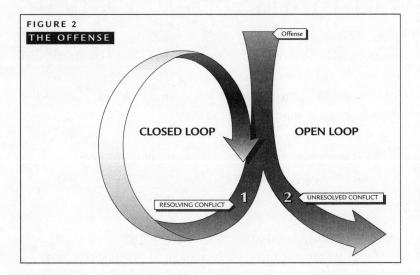

FIGURE 2
THE OFFENSE

Offense

CLOSED LOOP — OPEN LOOP

RESOLVING CONFLICT — 1 — 2 — UNRESOLVED CONFLICT

Barb and I often meet these husbands and wives after the Novocain of naïveté wears off. The glow of the honeymoon and first year of marriage has begun to fade. They come face-to-face with the reality that their spouse isn't a perfect angel. He or she has weaknesses and character flaws. He or she makes mistakes and acts selfishly. And as misunderstandings arise and shortcomings begin to surface in a variety of ways, each partner feels the sting of being offended.

Nancy's adulterous relationship with this other man deeply wounded her husband, Dean, and we all understand why. Adultery is a marital offense in the first degree. But there are a myriad of less serious ways we wrong our spouses. Perhaps you recognize some of the following examples from your own marriage.

* You forget your anniversary or another date important to your spouse.
* Your spouse makes a critical comment about your appearance.
* You promise to be home at a certain time but arrive an hour late.
* Your spouse is careless with a "treasure" of yours and breaks it.
* You rarely compliment your spouse on his or her appearance.
* Your spouse acts unappreciative of all you do for him or her.
* You withhold information from your spouse.
* Your spouse balks at doing anything you want to do.
* You leave things lying around when your spouse has asked you not to.
* Your spouse refuses to discipline the children when you are away.
* You bad-mouth your spouse in front of your children.
* Your spouse lies to you about the family finances.
* You ignore your spouse's friends.
* Your spouse lectures you when you really need comfort and understanding.

- ❀ You won't talk through problems with your spouse.
- ❀ Your spouse abuses you verbally.
- ❀ You spurn your spouse's approach to you sexually.

This list could drag on for many pages, of course. It's not meant to be an exhaustive catalog of marital offenses, merely a reminder that a wide variety of conflicts open loops of offense and hurt in every marriage, perhaps more frequently than we care to admit. Barb and I are not implying a fatalistic view of marital conflicts—they are going to happen anyway, so why try to prevent them. Rather, you should continue to work just as diligently to avoid unnecessary conflicts in your marriage as you do to resolve the conflicts and heal the hurts that occasionally happen.

Where do marital conflicts come from? Understanding the origins of the conflicts you experience at home will better equip you to deal with them. Barb will provide some valuable insight into why you and your spouse sometimes conflict.

THE ORIGINS OF MARITAL CONFLICTS

Conflict in marriage is inevitable because each couple brings two distinct lifestyles into the relationship. As husband and wife adjust to living together, those differences can lead to all kinds of problems. For example, how long did it take you to discover that one of you is a "morning glory" and the other is a "night owl"? Gary is the early riser in our home and I'm definitely the night owl. I usually come to bed a lot later than Gary, and if I wake him in the process, Mr. Nice Guy turns into Mr. Grouchy. Gary rises much earlier than I do, but if he gets a little too noisy, even whistling a happy tune in the bathroom, he's liable to hear from a very unhappy wife!

Let's look at a number of common differences that can lead to conflict and offenses in a marriage relationship.

Family Background Differences

Ron hails from the Pacific Northwest, and Ann grew up in the Southeast region of the country. They met in California as new employees of a large company. They never imagined that their differing family backgrounds would be a source of conflict in their marriage.

Ron's father was a successful salesman whose income increased steadily as Ron grew up. The family wasn't rich, but they enjoyed a comfortable lifestyle. They lived in a large suburban home, took trips around the country, and maintained a vacation cabin on the beach.

Ann spent her first few years on a farm before the family moved to a large southern city. Her father worked in a factory. He didn't earn big money, but the family wasn't poor. They had a roof over their heads, plenty to eat, and enough money in the bank to take care of future needs. When they vacationed, it was never more than 300 miles from home.

Ron enjoyed a very secure home life. His parents loved each other, and they helped their children any way they could. Ron's stable extended family was an additional source of his sense of security.

Ann characterizes her childhood years as alternately secure and chaotic. Her parents loved her and her two sisters, but they fought with each other and struggled through some tough times during Ann's childhood. They never divorced, but they were far from solid role models for how a couple should love and appreciate each other. Some members of Ann's extended family battled alcoholism, and some marriages ended in divorce.

The only time Ron's and Ann's families met was at their wedding. Today Ron and Ann live in the Midwest, far from both families. Their differing backgrounds have sparked conflict in their marriage. For example, Ron's family spends more money on Christmas gifts than Ann's family, and Ron feels the pressure to keep up the tradition. But Ron and Ann are on a limited budget.

More than once he has offended Ann by wanting to spend more on his parents than they spend on hers.

They also disagree about where to spend the holidays. Each of them loves to "go home," but distance of travel makes it impossible to visit both families at Christmas. Ron told Ann that he doesn't like going to her parents' home because "there's too much chaos and cigarette smoke." Ann is hurt by his attitude. She feels Ron should learn to live with the situation because she's not sure how many more years she will be able to spend Christmas with her elderly parents.

Ron and Ann are fortunate. Their faith in Christ and commitment to their relationship has helped them through many conflicts resulting from different family backgrounds. But for many of the couples Gary and I talk to, the clash of family values and traditions sparks major conflicts, heated arguments, and deep hurts year after year.

Personality Differences

It is said that opposites attract. In our experience, it is never more true than in the personality differences of married couples. We see the following combinations frequently. Perhaps you and your spouse fit into one or more of these examples.

- An outgoing, life-of-the-party type marries a quiet bookworm.
- A "neat freak" marries a "slob."
- A listener marries a talker.
- A feeler marries a thinker.
- "On time every time" marries "I'll get there when I get there."
- A scatterbrain marries a detail-oriented person.
- An art and music lover marries a color-blind monotone.
- A disciplined saver marries a happy-go-lucky spendthrift.

During courtship, many couples see their personality differences as complementary. But after the wedding, sometimes those differences begin to grate on the nerves and lead to conflict. The extrovert resents the introvert's plea to leave the party early. The slob feels nagged by the neat freak who insists on "a place for everything and everything in its place." The punctual person is frazzled by a spouse who can't leave on time.

Gary and I think personality differences are a good thing. As someone has said, "If two people are exactly alike, one of them isn't necessary." But be alert to ways your personality type may be a source of irritation to your spouse.

Values Differences

As our society drifts further and further from its Judeo-Christian base, marital conflicts sparked by differing values, worldviews, and philosophies become more common. Even when both partners are committed Christians, differing views on some issues lead to offenses.

Molly and Tom met and fell in love as college students involved with a Christian group on campus. They were certain their shared beliefs would give them a solid foundation for marriage, and they were right. But for two years, the choice of where to attend church was a great source of pain.

Molly grew up in a small, traditional church, the only church she had ever attended. All her brothers and sisters continued attending even after they started families of their own. She loved her pastor and the old hymns she had known all her life. Tom, however, attended a large church in the same community that featured contemporary worship and a less formal atmosphere. He felt stifled by the traditional liturgy in Molly's church and thought the people needed to "loosen up and enjoy themselves a little in church."

When they married, Tom felt they should attend his church, and he was offended when Molly said she was uncomfortable there. Molly was upset that Tom failed to see the importance of continuing her family's legacy by attending her church. Eventually, their arguments moved beyond which church to attend to areas such as marriage roles. As the leader of the home, Tom wanted Molly to follow him to his church. Molly wasn't sure a husband's biblical leadership included telling his wife where to go to church. They also squabbled over which style of worship was more biblical. Molly criticized Tom's church for placing more emphasis on raising hands in worship than on evangelism.

You and your spouse may have similar values, especially when it comes to Christian faith and practice. But where those values differ, watch out for conflict.

Male and Female Differences

Whenever people talk about the differences between men and women, the debate often focuses on the cause of these differences: Is it "nature" or "nurture"? For our discussion, however, the cause is not as important as the fact that differences do exist. Dr. James Dobson discusses male-female differences in his timeless book *Straight Talk*:

> Anyone who doubts that males and females are unique should observe how they approach a game of Ping-Pong or Monopoly or dominoes or horseshoes or volleyball or tennis. Women often use the event as an excuse for fellowship and pleasant conversation. For men, the name of the game is conquest. Even if the setting is a friendly social gathering in the host's backyard, the beads of sweat on each man's forehead reveal his passion to win. This aggressive competitiveness has been attributed to cultural influences. I don't believe it. As Richard Restak said, "At a birthday party for five-year-olds, it's not usually the girls who pull hair, throw punches, or smear each other with food."[2]

Men and women differ in many areas, but I'll mention one that commonly leads to offense and hurt: sexuality. Men are more quickly aroused and satisfied sexually than their wives. That's how they are wired. Women need more touching, caring, and relating. This one difference has complicated lovemaking throughout history. How often do husbands offend their wives by rushing through sex? How many women are hard-hearted and bitter because their husbands fail to meet their unique sexual needs? And how often do wives offend their husbands by withholding intercourse until the "atmosphere is just right"?

Gary Smalley and John Trent write in their book *Love Is a Decision:* "To most women, sex is much more than just an independent physical act. It's the culmination of a day filled with security, conversation, emotional and romantic experiences, and then, if all is right, sex. For the average man, you can reverse the order— or just skip everything that comes before sex!"[3]

Men, in order for your wife to fully enjoy the sexual experience, you need to meet her emotional needs as a woman. And wives, don't minimize your husband's need for the physical expression of sexual intimacy, even when he is slow to meet your emotional and relational needs.

As you can see, conflicts between husband and wife are inevitable, and they can arise from a number of seemingly innocent sources. These collisions of different lifestyles, combined with our weakness and sinfulness, give us plenty of ammunition for offending our spouses. But the offense is just the first step to opening the loop. In the next chapter, we will look at the next two stages in the chain reaction of conflict: hurt and anger.

The Chain Reaction
of Hurt and Anger

During a fitful night of sleep several years ago, I awoke and rolled over to find the light on in the hallway outside our bedroom. Barb wasn't lying next to me, so I knew something was wrong—and I had a good idea I was the cause of it. Earlier that evening we had experienced a conflict. While trying to resolve our problem, we argued. As I scrambled to defend my ego, I pulled out a subtle verbal zinger and shot it her way, something that fell out of my mouth before I thought through it. I knew it offended her, but she gamely carried on the discussion. I hoped she would quickly forget about my unkind remark.

The cool sheets on Barb's side of the bed alerted me that she hadn't forgotten. I slipped out of bed and went looking for her. I found her in the guest bedroom—alone, wounded, and tearful. It had been a long, painful night for the one I had promised to love, honor, and cherish. My thoughtless, defensive zinger had hit its mark. This was not one of the high points in a good marriage that is growing into a great marriage. I had opened a loop by offending Barb with my words. It was one of the many times Dr. Rosberg, the marriage counselor, had to take some of his own medicine by closing the loop and healing the hurt I had caused.

When you offend your spouse or your spouse offends you, it hurts. The pain is not so much physical as emotional and relational, although unhealed inner hurts can affect how you feel physically. Barb will give you a closer look at the dynamic of hurt in the open loop of marriage conflict and introduce where it can lead.

UNRESOLVED OFFENSES CAUSE HURT

When Gary "zinged" me that evening with an unkind remark, it hurt. But I didn't want him to see how much pain I felt, so I tried to ignore it. And when Gary didn't step in and close the loop right away, I felt even worse. Inside I was heartsick. I couldn't sleep that night. Slipping away to the guest bedroom, I cried from the inner pain I felt.

Now, in case this sounds one-sided, let me assure you that I am just as guilty of offending and hurting my husband from time to time. We have a good marriage that is growing better every day. But we still hurt each other, just like you do. Our marriage continues to grow stronger because, when the offenses and hurts happen, we try hard to close the loop as soon as possible. It's one of the ways we are divorce-proofing our marriage.

If an offense between you and your spouse is dealt with immediately, the hurt is fleeting and without lasting consequences. For example, wives, let's say that, while on a trip together, you let slip a critical remark about your husband's driving. Suddenly you feel a moment of chilly silence between you. Realizing your offense, you say with sincerity, "I'm sorry, honey. That was unkind and unfair of me, and I didn't mean to hurt you. Will you forgive me?" Your husband warms to your apology and forgives you—and the hurt is virtually negated by closing the loop so quickly.

Sadly, however, most marital offenses are not dealt with so efficiently. Sometimes you don't realize that what you said or did offended your spouse, so you are oblivious to the hurt you caused. More often, as in Gary's personal example above, you know what you did was hurtful, but you are too hardheaded or embarrassed to own up to the offense. So you let it slide, giving time for your spouse to stew over what happened while the pain intensifies. It's as if your offense opened a flesh wound and your reluctance to resolve it right away allowed infection to set in.

Another reason emotional pain is sometimes overlooked is because, when you are offended, you may not recognize the hurt right away. Let's face it: There's no blood, no broken or dislocated limbs, and no discernable physical pain. Something your spouse said or did left you feeling a little down. On the surface, it may not have seemed like such a big deal. *Why am I feeling so off center?* you ask yourself. *Maybe I'm coming down with the flu.* It doesn't hurt like other pain we know, so we fail to classify it as pain.

Then again, you may recognize the inner hurt right away but try to hide it, just as I did that night when Gary zinged me. You don't want your spouse to know he or she has hurt you. You don't want to be seen as vulnerable. So you tough it out and act as if nothing happened. In the meantime, the inner wound only gets worse.

Whether you are aware of it or not, when you or your spouse opens a loop by wronging each other in some way, it triggers

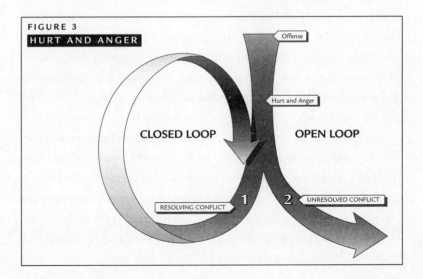

FIGURE 3
HURT AND ANGER

Offense

Hurt and Anger

CLOSED LOOP   OPEN LOOP

RESOLVING CONFLICT   1   2   UNRESOLVED CONFLICT

hurt, the primary emotion in a conflict. And if you delay closing the loop, that simmering inner hurt can boil over into anger. (See diagram in figure 3.)

UNHEALED HURT TRIGGERS ANGER

Anger is the next step in the open loop of conflict. We have learned that anger is a secondary emotion, typically following hurt, disappointment, or fear. It's what grows out of the offense and the hurt when they are not dealt with quickly. Unleashed anger only makes things worse in a conflict and becomes another hindrance to resolving it peacefully.

Anger is an emotion that Christians often try to deny. In public, we keep it in check. But in the privacy of our homes, we tend to let our defenses down and allow anger to build up and explode, often with grim consequences in the relationship.

In our conferences, when Gary and I talk about anger in a marriage relationship, we share what we call the "baked-potato syndrome." Picture a big, brown russet potato in the oven. You turn on the heat and the potato begins to warm. Given sufficient time, it bakes to a fluffy white inside, ready for butter, sour cream, chives, and bacon bits. But if you forget about the potato and let it bake too long, it could explode and make a mess in your oven. This illustrates what can happen when offenses, hurts, and anger are allowed to heat up through lack of loving action. The result can be a disaster.

Many counselors today say it is healthy to express our anger. Yes, it's good to express our feelings if we do it in a constructive way. We all know that when we are on the receiving end of uncontrolled anger, it gets ugly real fast. And if we are on the giving end, the guilt that follows is a reminder of just how messy a lack of self-control can become. The apostle Paul admonishes, "'Don't sin by letting anger gain control over you.' Don't let the sun go down while you are still angry, for anger gives a mighty foothold to the Devil" (Ephesians 4:26-27). Too often, however, we unleash anger as a weapon to retaliate for an unhealed hurt. When you release your anger with hostility and the intent to harm, it causes more problems than it solves.

You will be better equipped to deal with anger in your marriage if you understand the different types of anger and identify why you respond the way you do. Gary will provide further insight into the baked-potato syndrome.

WHAT TYPE OF ANGER HEATS UP IN YOU?

There are three varieties of the "baked potato" of anger: situational anger, displaced anger, and chronic anger. Each one has a different cause.

Some anger responses are *situational,* triggered by specific events. You can almost predict it: When a certain something happens, one of you reacts with anger. For example, Barb and I have identified several events that usually trigger anger in one or both of us. One situation that makes sparks fly is when Barb is behind schedule as we are leaving for church or an appointment. Sparks usually fly when we hang wallpaper or pictures together. Once I hang a picture, I don't want any more nail holes; one is enough. Barb, on the other hand, likes to experiment with different spots or later change things around. And I can get a little surly at Christmastime when I'm down on my hands and knees trying to get the tree to stand straight while my family is already starting to hang the ornaments.

What flips your anger switch? Perhaps one or more of the following scenarios tends to get you a little hot under the collar.

* Amy and Doug are happy together most of the time. But when he promises to be home by 6:00 P.M. for Amy's

chicken cordon bleu and doesn't arrive until 8:30, Amy blows a fuse.

* Frankie likes the way Celia always keeps their house tidy. She steps over the line, however, when she tries to organize Frankie's desktop in their home office. It drives Frankie up the wall.

* When they're out driving, Vic has to bite his tongue when Joella says something like, "You are going ten miles over the speed limit, Vic."

* Steve gets really ticked when Becky invites someone over for dinner without checking with him first. He's tempted to work late on purpose those nights.

* Patrick and Serina operate a home business and work well together. But whenever they paint or wallpaper a room in the house, Serina always gets mad at Patrick for his carelessness.

* Megan flies into a rage when she discovers that Reuben has been visiting pornographic Web sites. Every time he's caught, Reuben promises to quit. And with every new offense, Megan goes ballistic.

* Occasionally, it gets back to Antonio that Lucy has been sharing personal things about their marriage with her girlfriends. Whenever it happens, Antonio doesn't speak to her for a week.

Behind every eruption of situational anger are offenses and hurts that have not been resolved. The sooner you close the loop on offenses and hurts, the less damage you will suffer—or inflict—from anger.

Another variety of anger is one counselors refer to as *displaced anger*. Rather than confronting and dealing with the direct cause of the anger in a situation, the offended spouse expresses his or her feelings indirectly. Here are a couple of classic examples.

Your boss ticks you off at work, so you come home and yell at your spouse and kids for no reason. Or how about this classic: Your spouse offends you, so you go outside and kick the dog.

Tad understands displaced anger. Whenever he and Jeannie have a conflict, she "forgets" to buy his favorite snack at the market. The couple has been married thirteen years. Tad is an attorney and Jeannie is a chemical engineer. When a conflict arises in their home, Jeannie simply withdraws and does whatever Tad says, just as she and her mother did with Jeannie's domineering dad. She knows that if she stands up to Tad, he will just raise the volume until she gets the message of who is in control. So she backs off under the guise of being a submissive wife and vents her anger at him indirectly.

Tad loves a certain kind of pretzels. Before Jeannie goes to the market, he reminds her to pick up a package for him. She nods in agreement, but inside she reasons, *Sure, Tad, I'll buy the pretzels you want—as soon as you begin listening to me.*

The next day Tad goes to the cupboard to look for his pretzels and finds none. He asks, "Where are my pretzels, Jeannie?"

Jeannie replies in feigned innocence, "Oh, I'm sorry, honey, I forgot them. I'll remember next time." That's displaced anger. In her roundabout way, she is getting back at both her husband and her father for years of failing to listen to her heart.

Displaced anger may not be as damaging as other forms, but it still leaves a painful open loop in the relationship.

A third type of anger resulting from unhealed hurts is *chronic anger*. When an open loop is not closed in a timely manner, the hurt and anger are often shoved to the background and ignored. Because it is unresolved, this anger can flare up again and again. Buried wounds and anger generate an assortment of psychological and physical stresses that can ruin a person's perspective on life and eat away at the soul. People with chronic anger are like loose cannons, ready to blast away whenever someone unwittingly touches off the fuse.

Darlene is an example of chronic anger in a marriage. She was a cute, petite high school cheerleader when she started dating Todd, the star football player. Todd, a tough and very competitive linebacker, received a football scholarship to a nearby university. The couple was married after Todd's third year in college. Darlene had no clue that Todd's fierce drive to win would cast a pall over their life together.

Eighteen months into their marriage, Todd's actions let Darlene know that he was not going to take no for an answer when it came to sex. Whenever Darlene politely refused his romantic advances, Todd simply overpowered her until he got what he wanted. At first he made it seem like a game, but he played rough just like he did on the football field. If Darlene tried to resist physically, she got hurt. So she learned not to fight back, but she was seething inside. She felt cheap and disrespected.

Darlene knew only one word for what Todd was doing to her: abuse. But it wasn't something she dared to talk about with any of their friends or with her ladies' Bible study group at church. Whenever Todd started into his lovemaking routine, the hurt and anger flared up inside as she caved in to his pressure. Darlene attended every church retreat offered and organized "girls night out" sleepovers with her friends just to avoid climbing into bed with Todd.

For seventeen years, Darlene has displaced her chronic anger with compulsive eating. After a bad night, she heads straight for the refrigerator as soon as Todd leaves for work. The cute little high school cheerleader has ballooned to over two hundred pounds. But once or twice each week her unresolved anger rears its head once again and the cycle continues. As a Christian, she knows divorce is wrong. But she's not sure how much longer she can endure what is happening to her.

Offenses and hurts don't need to be as severe as Darlene's for chronic anger to cause great damage in your marriage. Don't take the risk. Learn to close the loop quickly and keep your marriage off the road to disconnect and emotional divorce.

How Do You Respond When Your Anger Heats Up?

Your personality type and your upbringing largely dictate just how you will respond when offenses cause hurts and hurts spark anger. We have noticed four types of people and responses to anger.

The Self-Protector. Self-protectors have a difficult time acknowledging that they have been hurt. Those who tend to stuff their anger act as if nothing is wrong or direct attention away from the offense. Expressing hurt requires vulnerability, so they deny the hurt to protect themselves from being vulnerable to further hurt.

Other self-protectors express their anger in an aggressive or hostile way rather than work through the offense that created the hurt. They lash out because they have discovered that the explosion helps to keep others at a distance, once again guarding against vulnerability and further hurt.

In a marriage relationship, a self-protecting spouse will either stuff anger and become passive-aggressive or let it fly in order to keep from exposing his or her heart to more hurt.

The Cannon. Some people explode with anger because it is a powerful weapon. In a disagreement or conflict, one person blows up and attacks the other person. When someone explodes in anger, it is difficult for most people to retaliate. They tend to back away because of their own insecurity. The cannon ends up "winning" the argument, not because his or her way is best but because the other person shrinks back and gives in. But when a cannon meets up with another cannon, the argument can escalate into a shouting match.

The Conformer. Greg and Tanya exemplify another group of people who either stuff or vent their anger. Greg is the exploder in their marriage, and Tanya is a stuffer. Both are conforming to lessons they learned from their culture or their families.

Greg conforms to the societal myth that "real men" are tough, independent, and never show emotion. It's what he learned by osmosis from his father, brothers, and the other men in his life. This false message states that it is not masculine for a man to admit that he has been hurt. You've heard some of the mottoes: "Big boys don't cry"; "Never let 'em see you sweat"; and the like.

Tanya grew up watching her mother repress her anger, even during continual verbal assaults from Tanya's father. Mom felt it was her duty as a Christian to acquiesce to her abusive husband. She never challenged his authority, even when he did not consult with her on important financial decisions.

As adults, Greg and Tanya find themselves acting out the parts that their families and their culture trained them to play. And they wonder why they can't resolve hurt and anger in their relationship.

The Denier. The fourth type of person dealing with anger is the denier. Amanda is a good example. Rather than expressing her hurt, she goes right to the anger stage. The problem is that she doesn't recognize when she is hurt, so she denies that there is a problem.

Amanda grew up in a home with parents who argued constantly and with two brothers who were always at each other's throats. Anger was the one emotion this family expressed. No one modeled for Amanda how to positively express hurt. Mom held her hurt inside. Amanda's brothers perceived themselves as "real men" raised by a dad who only knew how to show anger in a hostile way, so Amanda never saw hurt expressed by the men in her life. She used anger to stand her ground in a hostile environment where hurt was never legitimately expressed.

As an adult, Amanda developed patterns of unleashing her explosive anger at will. Other people kept their distance because her venting pushed them away. Amanda had a string of broken relationships with men. Whenever conflict occurred, she became hostile and denied that there were any problems.

When she finally married Judson, the fireworks started almost immediately. Every conflict resulted in an explosion and a denial. "I don't know what your problem is, Judson, but I don't have a problem," she would insist angrily. Her volatile anger has been a significant barrier to their intimacy and happiness. The more Amanda denies her hurt, the closer she and Judson drift toward separation.

How Will You Deal with Hurt and Anger?

Unless you and your spouse learn how to work through your hurt and anger, you will likely find yourself on an emotional roller coaster that never slows down. Stuffing anger into some dark corner of your heart may temporarily help you skirt past a conflict, but the anger doesn't go away. Venting anger through a verbal tirade, an argument, screaming, crying, or slamming doors may help you let off a little steam, but it won't solve the root problem and you will explode again and again. The longer you allow the cycles of stuffing and exploding to continue, the more you will hurt yourself and your spouse.

If you persist in stuffing your hurt and anger, it will affect you negatively in mind, body, and spirit. Your outlook on life will tarnish, your hope for deeper happiness in marriage will fade, and you will be more susceptible to illness. Unresolved anger evolves into bitterness and resentment. You see the world through distorted lenses. You become hardened and withdrawn, developing physical symptoms such as headaches, muscle aches, colitis, ulcers, compulsive behaviors, and scores of other problems. In the process, you pull away from your spouse and tumble toward the precipice of emotional and physical divorce.

The results from venting your anger are not any better. It still fosters a critical, bitter, and resentful attitude. And venting is no healthier than stuffing anger inside. Since venting does not resolve issues, you just get even more angry and entrenched in this destructive pattern. In the meantime, you will tend to alienate yourself from those closest to you: your spouse and children. Venting anger debilitates you, distances you from your spouse by keeping the loop open, and robs your marriage of joy and stability.

Much of the hurt and anger you experience in your marriage relationship are the result of unresolved conflicts between you and your spouse. They are all part of open loops, and the longer the loops remain open, the greater will be the turmoil in your marriage.

Closing every loop as soon as possible is vital to divorce-proofing your marriage. In part 3 of this book, Barb and I will coach you on the skills of resolving your conflicts, healing the hurts that happen between you, and disarming your anger. But first we need to expose the wrong ways to resolve conflict and the sources of these counterproductive messages.

Where Did You Learn to Resolve Conflict?

Kristen and Nicole sipped lattes at Starbucks during their usual Tuesday morning get-together. "Brian is driving me up the wall," Kristen complained. "He never talks to me and I don't know how to get through to him."

"I saw a segment about that on Dr. Phil a few weeks ago," Nicole replied. "And the psychologist said you resolve the issue by . . ."

⁓

The angry words had been flying hot and heavy between Wade and Kathleen for twenty minutes. Finally Kathleen said, "We're not getting anywhere by arguing. I think we need help sorting out our differences."

Wade nodded in agreement. "A guy at work said he and his wife read a book about marriage conflicts by an Eastern philosopher. It's not exactly a Christian book, but he claims it helped them a lot."

"Maybe we should give it a try," Kathleen suggested.

⁓

Bruce had just unloaded on his best friend, Rick. The subject was Bruce's wife, Tracy, and the many ways she made Bruce angry.

"I'm telling you, Bruce," Rick said, "you can't keep your anger bottled up inside. When Tracy ticks you off, tell her what you think in no uncertain terms. It may hurt her at the moment, but she'll get over it. I'm your friend, Bruce. Trust me on this. I was listening to that radio shrink, you know the woman everyone listens to. That's what she told a caller the other day."

As these brief scenes suggest, everybody knows something about resolving marital conflict. And there seems to be no shortage of information, instruction, and advice available to us on the subject. Whether you realize it or not, you came to your wedding day with certain conflict-resolution strategies that you accumulated consciously or subconsciously as you grew up and prepared for marriage. But you have probably discovered by now that some of those strategies are about as effective as bloodletting was for curing illness a couple of centuries ago.

Many individuals and couples wonder why it is so difficult to resolve conflicts in their marriages. Barb and I believe it is because they have never learned the right way to do it. They either received bad advice from someone, took their cues from the wrong role models, read books that contained more opinion than truth about forgiving love, or otherwise assimilated unproductive strategies for handling the conflict, hurt, and anger in their marriages. And in learning the wrong stuff, their conflicts have gone unresolved or become worse.

Where did you learn what you know about closing the loop of conflict? There are two primary sources through which most people get their information and advice on such matters: culture and family. Before you can learn the right way to heal the hurts in your marriage, you must realize what you have been doing wrong, identify where you got those patterns, and determine to let them go.

First, I will talk to you about the negative influences of our culture on conflict resolution. Later in the chapter, Barb will focus on the role our families sometimes play in blocking us from closing the loop.

WHAT OUR CULTURE TEACHES US ABOUT CONFLICT

There are a number of voices speaking out to us from our culture, influencing the way we think about conflicts with our spouses and how they should be handled. But since we live in a godless culture that minimizes biblical truth, these messages must be regarded as generally hostile to God's way of healing hurts. Here are just a few of the voices and what they are saying.

Messages from the Media

One Saturday morning, I asked Barb to accompany me to the bookstore to buy some magazines. I wanted to pick up the latest buzz from the world of pop psychology on how to resolve conflict. I was in a good mood as we headed into the store, but as I browsed through the contents pages of fifteen to twenty magazines, I found myself getting a little ticked. Some of the articles on relationships had titles like:

- Why I Date Your Husband
- Sleeping with the Enemy: How to Fight with the Man You Love
- Salvaging the Troubled Relationship: When It's Up to You
- Good Girls, Bad Girls
- Good Ways to Say Bad Things

I bought a handful of magazines and spent the next few days reading them. I didn't like what I found. No wonder so many couples struggle with unhealed hurts. Pop psychology, as perpetuated in the print media, is giving bad advice. Here are some examples:

* From *Mademoiselle* on the topic of fighting with the man you love: "It's not a party until someone breaks a glass, and it's not a relationship until you have a fight. In fact, the occasional lovers' brawl is an essential part of a successful romance. It's healthy. It's emotionally cleansing. Besides which, did you really think you could have all that steady sex at no cost? Of course not—you play, you pay."[1]

* From *Cosmopolitan* on the topic of salvaging the troubled relationship: "For many, the only choice is to start afresh with a more liberated male. But according to experts, you do have the power to bring a stubborn man to the negotiating table. . . . Overcome urges to play "good girl". . . . Earn and control your own money, make an unexpected sexual request, dress sexy—for you, carve out your own space, and develop your own quirks."[2]

* From *Cosmopolitan,* illustrating good ways to say bad things to your partner: "'You know, Chloe,' I said, 'I've always really loved the way you treat people. You're about as kind and considerate as Lady Macbeth on a "good" day.' Chloe said nothing, but her eyes were as wide and heartbreaking as Bambi's. Dinner was served. Then it was 'her' turn. 'There's something I've been meaning to tell you, Peter,' she said. 'The way you stuff your mouth with food compares favorably to a prisoner who's just been released from Devil's Island.'"[3]

The more I read, the worse it got. Magazine after magazine echoed our culture's hedonistic, self-centered approach to relationships. And you find the same message in so many books in the self-help section at the bookstore. It pervades our culture. Here are some of the key messages bombarding us:

- ❊ Look out for number one.
- ❊ If there's a problem in your relationship, walk away.
- ❊ If the relationship you're in isn't satisfying, get out and find another one.
- ❊ There are no moral rights or wrongs. You need to decide what's right for you.

The print media are powerful, convincing weapons of propaganda. The books and magazines of so-called authorities are the sources that millions of men and women use as a guideline for dealing with relational hurts and conflicts. However, in our culture television dwarfs the influence of the printed page. You probably internalized a number of unhealthy concepts for resolving conflicts from the television programs you have watched over the years.

You can make a strong case that the dramatic rise in the divorce rate in America since 1960 is directly related to the proliferation of our culture's message on morals and relationships through the medium of television. We are a culture addicted to the tube. Studies document the staggering number of hours children, youth, and adults spend watching television. The programs and commercials we absorb play a huge part in determining our thinking and behavior. And when the programs emanating from the tube are filled with wrong messages about how to relate to people and resolve conflicts, is it any wonder so many people enter marriage with big gaps in their emotional and social skills?

Take, for example, one of the staples of daytime television—the talk show. To be fair, a few hosts occasionally present helpful, healthy ways to heal relationships. But these programs are outnumbered by the scores of programs that sensationalize conflict and provoke on-stage arguments—even brawls. A steady diet of talk shows—especially the numerous "shock talk" shows—fill the viewer's mind with counterproductive images and messages about resolving conflict: Take care of yourself first, strike back when you are hurt, don't let your spouse off the hook, and get out when you can't get along.

If you can't find a talk show to watch during the daylight hours, you can certainly find a soap opera. But the message and modeling about conflict resolution is even less helpful on the soaps than on the talk shows. Lying, back-stabbing, infidelity, hatred, and revenge between spouses is the daily fare. It doesn't get any better on prime-time television in the evening. Inane sitcoms try to make us laugh about conflicts, and high-powered dramas cause us to wonder if TV producers know anything at all about healthy relationships.

When you feed on a steady diet of television each day and then a conflict with your spouse rears its ugly head at bedtime, what do you rely on to resolve it? Do you allow it to escalate into a shouting match or worse like the couples on TV? Do you follow the harebrained advice of a celebrity or so-called expert from a talk show? Do you make a big joke of it like the sitcoms do? Do you storm away and seek consolation with another man or woman—emotionally, physically, or through pornography—as they do on daytime and prime-time dramas? You likely will not act out everything you watch, but the words and images you take in from TV can color your response to conflict.

One significant element to healing marital hurts is all but missing from television programming: God. Unless you're watching a Christian station—and you even need to be discerning about which religious programs you watch—you rarely hear anything resembling a healthy, biblical solution to the pain of the human heart. Barb and I are not advocating that you have a garage sale to get rid of your TVs. But we do caution you that most of what you see on TV relating to healing marital hurts is steeped in the secularism and me-ism of today's culture.

Messages from People You Trust

Have you noticed that when you and your spouse are in conflict, it's sometimes easier to talk to someone else about it? We all need to vent our feelings, talk about our frustrations, and seek advice. That's what friends and family are for. And we often trust our loved ones implicitly, regarding their advice as gospel.

The problem is that many of the people we trust have grown up hearing the same cultural messages about resolving marital hurts that we have. They may have the same kinds of unresolved conflicts in their own marriages. Since they care about you, these well-meaning friends end up parroting the culture's watchwords of self-protection: leave, fight back, call an attorney, you don't deserve it, take care of yourself, or make him or her pay.

At the core of your friends' advice is their concern that you not get hurt. That's why they may urge you to create some distance between you and your spouse. Pulling back may alleviate one kind of pain, but consistently avoiding conflict leads to the death of a marriage, which hurts infinitely more than working through the conflict. If your friends or other family members are after you to give up on your spouse or get out of the relationship, they may think they have your best interest at heart, but they are not giving you wise counsel.

Another source of advice for resolving hurts is the professional counselor. I know about this world because marriage and family therapy is my profession. But I also know the pitfalls of "humanistic counseling," in which I and most counselors were trained. We were taught that human beings are basically good and that, when the counselor provides a positive orientation for change, people will seek the good in themselves and become the best they can be.

They just need to look inside themselves and rely on their innate goodness to solve their problems. And if that doesn't work, they just need to alter behavior to bring about positive change. It took me about three weeks in practice as a new counselor to begin to reject that belief system.

I am deeply concerned about the impact my training had on me. As I often say, the further I get from my training, the better off I believe I am. Not because my professors were bad people or poor educators, because they were neither. The problem is that humanistic counseling discourages both client and therapist from centering on the ultimate source of change that heals: Jesus Christ. Secular counselors provide therapy from a secular perspective. They regard the idea that people were created to have a relationship with a living God as part of the client's problem instead of the very answer to our deepest relational needs. But to conduct therapy without God and the Bible is like jumping on a trampoline without a spotter. Nobody is there to catch you.

Can Christians benefit from counseling with a non-Christian? Yes, in some rare instances, as long as you realize that the counselor's worldview and approach to healing may be totally different from yours. Some of the methods for resolving conflict taught by secular counselors are good; some are not. One ingredient that is often missing is forgiveness. As you will discover in part 3 of this book, forgiveness is a key step in healing hurts from a biblical perspective. Yet this step is often ignored altogether in the secular world. With that in mind, you need to filter the secular counselor's advice through your biblically based belief system.

Unfortunately, some Christian counselors are as ineffective as their unbelieving counterparts. Why? Because often when they purport to counsel from a Christian perspective, there is actually little emphasis on a biblical or spiritual orientation. You may need to go to several counselors before you discern, through seeking God's mind and heart, that one particular counselor is the best fit for you. I know this process can be disconcerting, but it is better to have a series of initial appointments with several counselors than to sign on for long-term counseling with someone who does not lead you to a healthy and biblical restoration of your relationship.

Messages from the Church

It may seem hard to believe, but sometimes the church disseminates information about healing marital hurts that is contrary to the teaching of the Bible. Rarely do church leaders mislead their congregations intentionally; they are probably only teaching as they have been taught. But since these voices carry the weight of authority, many people assume what they are hearing is 100 percent correct.

Take, for example, the issue of headship and submission in marriage. Many Christian leaders, especially men, point to Paul's teaching in Ephesians 5:24 to support the view that men should dominate their wives and that wives should submit to their decisions in any conflict or difference of opinion. The verse reads: "As the church submits to Christ, so you wives must submit to your husbands in everything."

A man who is interested only in absolute control over his wife will stop there. He will rarely go on to the next six verses that help us understand that headship is not about a husband dominating his wife but serving her:

And you husbands must love your wives with the same love Christ showed the church. He gave up his life for her to make her holy and clean, washed by baptism and God's word. He did this to present her to himself as a glorious church without a spot or wrinkle or any other blemish. Instead, she will be holy and without fault. In the same way, husbands ought to love their wives as they love their own bodies. For a man is actually loving himself when he loves his wife. No one hates his own body but lovingly cares for it, just as Christ cares for his body, which is the church. And we are his body. (Ephesians 5:25-30)

My friend Robert Lewis describes the difference between a "lording leader" and a "servant leader" in his book *Rocking the Roles*. Here's his description of a lording leader:

The lording leader loves to give orders. He's the boss. He has to have control. He makes all the decisions; everyone else just carries out his directives. If anyone questions his decisions, he silences them with another string of commands. That's because he's not interested in questions, suggestions, or better ideas. He's only interested in action, in getting things done his way. . . . The lording leader becomes defensive when his wife challenges him with her own thoughts and view. He views everything from a win/lose perspective. He can't stand to be wrong and let his wife be right. He certainly can't admit to her when he's wrong. So he browbeats her into going along with him, and manipulates her into granting his wishes.[4]

Barb and I have seen many marriages damaged by husbands who used their role as the head of the home to rule their wives with an iron fist of control. This unbiblical view can cause long-term bitterness and damage to the relationship as well as harm a wife's relationship to God. When I coach men on servant leadership, I talk about "out-serving" their wives in order to bring honor to the relationship. Out-serving means that a man intentionally puts himself lower than his wife by loving her, honoring her, and cherishing her with a servant's heart. When he does, her trust in him will grow and she will feel secure in responding to and supporting him.

Each of the messages from our culture is loud, persistent, and persuasive. But, at times, there is an even more influential voice speaking about marital conflict and how to resolve it. Barb will now share with us the kinds of messages we receive from our families.

WHAT OUR FAMILIES TEACH US ABOUT CONFLICT

For Gary and me, home is really where the heart is. When we think of our families of origin, we remember the love and camaraderie, holiday dinners, birthday celebrations, vacations, times when we laughed together and cried together. We also remember parents who were committed to getting along with each other, talking—and listening—to each other, and settling their differences.

Gary's parents were married fifty-four years before God called his dad, John, home. My parents have been married sixty-two years as I write this, and they are still celebrating a godly marriage. When it comes to commitment to the permanence of marriage, Gary and I have both been blessed with great role models, not only with marriages that have gone the distance, but also with joyful and fulfilling marriages. When it comes to dealing with conflict and hurt in our relationship, our families were a positive and helpful influence.

Sadly, not all people can say this about their families. For many people, the very mention of family or parents sparks other memories—absence, loss, pain. Conflicts and pain at home were frequent, and forgiveness and healing were infrequent or absent altogether. And these people have carried what they learned at home into their marriages. Unfortunately, they don't realize how they are perpetuating the same problems with their own spouses and children. It's not until they end up in a counselor's office, trying to sort out the messes of their marriages, that they are willing to take a hard look at themselves to discern why they act as they do.

You have probably noticed people who are repeating behavior patterns, both good and bad patterns, that they learned from their parents. A woman mirrors the perfectionism she once hated in her mother. A man finds solace in rage and control, just as his father did. A boy tries to win the approval of a father who never seemed satisfied with even the greatest accomplishments, and then he grows up to place the same unrealistic demands on his own children. Of all the married couples we counsel who are having difficulties resolving conflict, the vast majority need to come to terms with unhealthy patterns they learned during childhood.

When Gary and I consider the differences in families and the impact of these differences on resolving conflict, we often think of a parable Jesus taught. Here's how it goes:

> A farmer went out to plant some seed. As he scattered it across his field, some seeds fell on a footpath, and the birds came and ate them. Other seeds fell on shallow soil with underlying rock. The plants sprang up quickly, but they soon wilted beneath the hot sun and died because the roots had no nourishment in the shallow soil. Other seeds fell among thorns that shot up and choked out the tender blades. But some seeds fell on fertile soil and produced a crop that was thirty, sixty, and even a hundred times as much as had been planted. Anyone who is willing to hear should listen and understand! (Matthew 13:3-9)

In this parable, which illustrates how the condition of the soil can affect the fruitfulness of the harvest, Jesus is talking about the differences between human hearts. But we also believe the four soils can represent different types of families and how they respond to conflict. I wonder if you will recognize your family of origin, or your present marriage and family, in one of these four descriptions.

The Good Family

Have you ever said about a neighbor, "The Andersons are such good people! They're an impressive couple, and they have a lovely family. Everyone likes them."

We all have neighbors like the Andersons, don't we? They're really nice people, the salt of the earth. They make a good living and keep their lawns mowed and trimmed. They treat their kids well. They vote every election day. Some may even attend church and be highly moral people. And they are always ready to loan a gardening tool to their neighbors. There's only one thing missing from many good couples like the Andersons: They lack a personal relationship with Jesus.

These kinds of people are like the hard-packed soil where the seed cannot take root. They may have heard the message of the gospel but have never let it penetrate their hearts. They either don't recognize their need for a relationship with Jesus (because the voices of our culture are drowning out the truth), or they hear it and don't care. They turn a deaf ear to the truth and decide to live their lives just for themselves, casting off "church stuff" as either an encumbrance from their parents' generation or as hype from a bunch of "religious nuts."

This is perhaps the most difficult home of all to understand because the family members may not realize how needy they are. Perhaps you or your spouse grew up with parents who were good to you but who did not provide a spiritual foundation for the family.

How do "good" families deal with conflict? They teach and model what appears to be a healthy strategy: Fight fair, negotiate, and compromise in order to get what is rightfully yours. It sounds good until you look at the basis for this philosophy. We call it the fifty-fifty relationship. The message each family member delivers in this arrangement is, "I'll do my part if you do your part." Life becomes a matter of trade-offs and compromises, with parents and kids keeping score so one person never gets or gives more than the other.

In this kind of home we see a lack of serving because family members have no place for the loving, serving Savior. Instead, we see a strong emphasis on self-centered people trying to get what they deserve. Kids tend to grow up to be me-oriented adults. When they leave their parents' homes for their own marriages, they bring these values along with them. So when it comes to resolving conflict, these people are primarily looking out for themselves. They will be drawn to more of a contractual style of marriage, focusing on what they *get,* rather than a covenantal style of marriage, focusing on what they *give.* Little healing can happen when one or both partners are so self-centered.

The Religious Family

The Bensons live down the street from the Andersons. In many ways they resemble their neighbors—at least from the outside. The Bensons are good, moral people, but they are also religious. They believe in God, attend church, and try to follow the Ten Commandments. But there is no personal relationship with God. Christianity for them is a religious ritual. The Bensons represent the rocky soil where the seed dies for lack of depth.

The religious home is shallow and without root. Their faith is a toxic faith. Christianity is a set of rules, a code to live by. Parents like this remind us of the Pharisees in the New Testament. They were religious people who professed to know the truth about God, but it was all superficial. Their goal was to gain attention and applause—and Jesus called them on it.

Because of the emphasis on rules, the Bensons live by a rigid structure of family roles. Dad runs the family with an iron fist, demanding respect from his wife and children. The watchword in a religious home is "Do what you're told." The Bible is used as a club to alter behavior. Conflicts are either avoided out of fear or "settled" quickly as the kids fall into line with Dad and Mom's dictums. Authoritarian parents are harsh and demanding. The kids may toe the line externally, but often their spirits are broken by such harshness. Or deep inside they are seething with rebellion, just waiting for a chance to escape the religious tyranny.

How will the Benson children grow up to view God? Typically they will see him as waiting in the wings to catch them doing something wrong so he can punish them. How will they see their dad? He is the czar of the family, fully in charge and never to be questioned. How about their mom? She may be seen as the compliant, passive woman who keeps quiet so she won't rock the boat.

As adults, these children tend to bring one of three types of behavior patterns into their own marriages. One, they may become overly compliant, doing what they are supposed to do out of sheer duty. When it comes to resolving conflicts and healing hurts, they are more interested in keeping the peace than in dealing with issues. Two, they may rebel against God, church, and rules. Conflicts usually get worse—not better—in this environment. Three, they may become indifferent, both to God and to their spouses. As such, conflicts often go unresolved and hurts unhealed.

Is there hope for those who have been raised in the rigidity of a legalistic home? Definitely. These people can develop a healthy relationship with God that is free from the punitive attitudes they experienced as children. They can learn that a balanced and healthy faith focuses on the God of the Bible, not on the distortion others have constructed by putting God in a box and limiting him to a bunch of rules. And they can develop a sensitivity to offenses in the marriage relationship and a willingness to heal them.

The Wounded Family

The Carters live a few blocks away from the Andersons and the Bensons. They are not what you would call good people. The parents are controlling and abusive toward each other and toward the children. This is the kind of soil where anything of God or goodness is choked out by anger, hatred, spite, and distrust. Their kids are growing up never quite feeling accepted and loved the way God intended.

Gary and I often refer to the adult children from homes like the Carters' as the "walking wounded." These people were hurt by growing up in homes with serious relational problems. Some bear the emotional—and sometimes physical—scars of alcohol and drug abuse, emotional and physical abuse, or sexual abuse in the home. Others are wounded in less obvious ways. Some were raised without the love and nurture they needed because their parents were so distracted by their own wounds. Still others were wounded by the loss of a parent through death or divorce. Whatever the root cause of their pain, these families tend to raise kids that carry the pain of the parents into the next generation.

Wounded people often struggle when it comes to dealing with their own marital conflicts. That's the way it was for Megan and Ben. Whenever they began to argue, Ben got angry and Megan ran to the bedroom, telling Ben by the slam of the door that she needed some space. In the meantime, Ben wanted to resolve the issue right away. The more Megan pulled away, the more Ben demanded that they "fix" the problem.

After describing the situation to Gary in a counseling session, Megan commented, "That's just the way it is, Dr. Rosberg."

Gary asked, "Do you ever sense, Megan, that you are repeating the same old pattern that you saw growing up?"

After a moment of contemplative silence, she corrected herself. "No, that's just the way it *was* when I was growing up." Megan had suddenly realized she was acting just like her mom.

Megan's father was an alcoholic with violent mood swings. When he and his wife argued, he got angry, swore at her, and sometimes struck her. Over time, Megan's mother learned that the best way to avoid violence was to let him have his way. She withdrew and did whatever she could to please him. Megan was following the same pattern, withdrawing from Ben at the first hint of anger. She knew her behavior hindered healing in her relationship with Ben. But she didn't know what to do about it until she discovered that she was mimicking the pattern she had seen in her wounded family. Once she made that connection, Gary was able to help her develop ways to resolve her conflicts with Ben instead of retreat.

If you came from a wounded family, we offer the same hope to you. It is never too late to learn effective ways to deal with the conflicts in your marriage.

The Biblical Family

The Duncans represent the biblical home. They live in the same neighborhood as the Bensons, Andersons, and Carters. What makes them different? They have problems and conflicts just like the other three couples. But like the good soil in the parable, their fertile hearts have allowed the truth of God's Word to take root, so they are better equipped to appropriate God's healing for the hurts in their family. Rather than let conflicts drive a wedge between them, they allow those difficulties to pull them together for healing and growth.

Here's what a typical conflict looks like in the Duncan household. Does it look anything like the family you grew up in? Does it look anything like your family today?

"Erin, you eat your spaghetti like such a pig," Rachel snarled at her sister across the dinner table.

"Dad, did you hear what Rachel called me?" Erin whined. "A pig!" Then she snatched up her plate and stomped into the family room to finish her dinner alone.

"Rachel, why did you say that?" Dad said. "You know Erin is sensitive about comments like that. A nice, reasonably quiet dinner was just spoiled."

"But, Dad, didn't you see her slurping up spaghetti? Her face was almost in her plate! The way she eats is gross."

When Dad and Mom came into the family room, they could tell that Erin had been wounded by her big sister's attack and the apparent indifference of her parents. They knew a loop had been opened and that they needed to talk about it as a family. So they called Rachel into the room.

As they talked it through together, the real issue came to light. Mom and Dad learned that Erin felt self-conscious about her weight, interpreting Rachel's comment as "You eat as much as a *fat* pig." Rachel, sensing that her words had really stung her sister, realized that the hurt went deep, far deeper than she ever intended. She apologized and said she was referring to Erin's manners, not her weight. Erin forgave her sister. As they talked and listened to each other, the conflict dissipated.

Mom added, "Girls, do you see how you can really hurt each other with your words? We all need to be careful how we talk to each other. This is also good for Dad and me to remember, because we sometimes get sharp with each other when things are not going smoothly." Over the next several minutes, the Duncans experienced genuine forgiveness and healing in their relationships.

If you grew up in a family like the Duncans, you have experienced something of the biblical pattern for healing hurts in your marriage and family. But even if your parents were not like Dad and Mom Duncan, you can learn to resolve conflict if you recognize the need for the presence of the living God who helps us to heal from the inside out. And you are not confined to the patterns you have learned from our culture and your family, as Gary will explain in the next section.

WHAT TO DO ABOUT WHAT YOU LEARNED

For many years now, Barb and I have heard a litany of familiar complaints from husbands and wives who came into their marriages negatively influenced by our culture and their families of origin. Speaking of their own marriages and hurts, they say things like: "I just don't know how to do this right"; "I grew up in a dysfunctional home, so I don't know what normal is"; "No one ever taught me how to deal with conflicts"; "My parents' example is so ingrained in me, I'll never be able to change."

You may feel the same hopelessness, the same inability to change. You may feel destined to live out the same ineffective patterns in your own marriage. But that's like giving up on a garden because the soil is too hard or too rocky or infested with weeds. Have you ever heard of a pick, shovel, hoe, soil amendments, and a little hard work? In the same way you can change the condition of soil and unlearn bad patterns of dealing with conflict and learn new ones. It's never too late to learn and implement the biblical principles for forgiving love.

It is our God-given responsibility to cultivate good soil in our marriage relationships so that our children and grandchildren will have a biblical pattern to follow in their marriages. The psalmist wrote: "For [God] issued his decree to Jacob; he gave his law to Israel. He commanded our ancestors to teach them to their children, so the next generation might know them—even the children not yet born—that they in turn might teach their children. So each generation can set its hope anew on God, remembering his glorious miracles and obeying his commands" (Psalm 78:5-7). As you divorce-proof your marriage through forgiving love, you will help your children to divorce-proof their marriages.

So what are you doing to alter the patterns you learned? How are you making your marriage different from that of your parents? How can you bequeath to your children a family legacy that is more biblical and positive than that of your family of origin? You can look at this responsibility in two ways. You can think of it as a tremendous burden and a lot of hard work. Or you can welcome it as an opportunity to pass on to your children something that was not passed on to you. Even if you did not grow up in a healthy home, you can commit yourself to developing healthy patterns for resolving conflict.

The family you came from is important, but it is not as important as the family you will leave behind. Identify from your family of origin the barriers to communication and healthy conflict resolution. Gain whatever insight you can from the past, deal with the emotional pain of it, and then move on to developing new patterns that include confession and forgiveness of offenses and healing of hurts. As you leave the past behind and begin to create a more positive present, you will bless the next generation. One way or another, you will leave your handprints all over the personalities and hearts of your children. Will you leave behind a generation that will reach the world for Christ, or will you give up at the daunting task and let them go their own way?

When our older daughter, Sarah, was born in 1978, I read in the newspaper that I could anticipate spending about $80,000 for four years of college education when she grew up. I about choked on my breakfast cereal that morning. Eighty thousand dollars! At the time, I was earning about $12,000 per year as a probation officer. But we started saving, and somehow Sarah's college expenses were covered.

You may also have a plan for your child's education. But what are you doing to give your children the spiritual training and skills they will need for their lives and marriages? What kind of godly heritage are you leaving them? The key is found in establishing a home that honors God, a home where each individual is encouraged to develop a relationship with Jesus, a home where people make mistakes and fail each other but recognize they have the power, through God, to be transformed.

Conflict in your marriage is inevitable, but you are not trapped in the dysfunctional patterns of resolving conflict you learned from your parents or the world around you. If you grew up in a painful situation, we will coach you on how to break out of your negative behaviors and begin a new pattern of resolving conflicts. In parts 2 and 3 of this book, Barb and I will provide you with a viable option for responding to the open loops of conflict, anger, and hurt. Whenever you discover an open loop of conflict, first you must make a decision about how you will respond to it. In part 2 we will work through the choices with you.

PART II

THE FORK
IN THE ROAD

What Is Your Conflict-Resolution Style?

It's a beautiful spring day, the kind that beckons you to drop what you're doing inside and head outside. So you may do something that Barb and I enjoy doing: take off for a walk in the woods. As you traipse down the lane, you hear the birds chirping and see two squirrels chasing each other. You carefully dodge the ruts in the path, leftovers from the winter's snow and ice. You can't help but hum a happy tune as you see the sun breaking through the trees, its rays dancing off the leaves around you.

Then you come to an unexpected fork in the road. It's decision time. To your left is a well-traveled, paved pathway. Everybody else seems to be on it: joggers, walkers, skaters, and cyclists. It must be the popular way to go, though it is jammed with traffic. To the right is a narrow, leaf-strewn path illuminated by the sunlight and winding into the woods. You don't see anyone else on the path, but it invites you, as if the light is showing you the way. Which way should you go?

There are many forks in the road of day-to-day living. Sometimes we don't even see the intersection. We just put our heads down and charge ahead on the road most traveled. At other times we slow down and wonder which way we want to go. And still other times we come to a full stop and ask the tough question: Which way do I really *need* to go?

Every time you open a loop of conflict in your marriage—

whether it is a major argument or just a minor difference of opinion—you stand at a fork in the road. Once an offense has led to hurt and hurt has turned to anger, you are faced with two choices. You can (1) choose to resolve the conflict and close the loop, or (2) choose not to resolve the conflict and leave an open loop (see the diagram in figure 4).

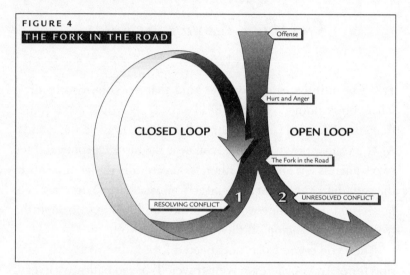

FIGURE 4
THE FORK IN THE ROAD

Offense

Hurt and Anger

CLOSED LOOP   **OPEN LOOP**

The Fork in the Road

RESOLVING CONFLICT   1   2   UNRESOLVED CONFLICT

You may come to this fork in the road with your spouse several times a week or several times a day. Some of the following scenes may jog your memory:

* You and your spouse are at the paint store picking out new paint for your bedroom. When your spouse casually mentions to the clerk that you will be doing the painting, you stiffen inside. You never volunteered for that job. Besides, you already have a list of household projects that will take you the next ten weekends to complete. The more you think about your spouse's comment, the angrier you get.
* It was just a simple statement, but you heard your

spouse's hurt behind it: "We haven't been out together, just the two of us, in more than a month."

✻ You happen to be the one to open the credit card statement this month, and what you find irritates you. Your spouse made two expensive purchases last month that were outside the budget parameters you two had agreed upon. What's worse, your spouse never consulted you about them.

✻ You look all over the house for your favorite, comfy, old slippers. When you ask about them, your spouse says, "Oh, those ratty old things? I tossed them into the trash last week."

✻ Earlier in the evening, your spouse hinted about making love tonight. You're not in the mood, but instead of saying something, you slip into bed a half hour early and pretend to be asleep when your spouse joins you. You can hear the sigh of disappointment from the other side of the bed.

In conflicts like these, and the many other kinds you face, you need to make a decision. Will you follow your natural inclination in the situation—which is probably to ignore or delay closing the loop, or will you trust God and take responsibility for attempting to resolve the conflict? Keep in mind that the old axiom applies here: Not to decide is to decide. As long as you do *not* make a choice to close the loop, you are deciding *not* to resolve the conflict.

In these three chapters, Barb and I want to talk to you about this important fork in the road and why it may be difficult for you to make the right choice to resolve the conflict and heal the attending hurts. In this chapter, we will help you understand how your present style of responding to conflict may indeed hinder your efforts to close the loop.

YOUR CONFLICT-RESOLUTION STYLE

Closing the loop in marital conflicts is never simple or easy. One reason is that each of us tends to react to hurt and anger in one of several different styles. As we discussed in chapter 4, your style for dealing with conflict is likely to be the product of what you learned in your family of origin and what you have adopted from our culture. And since these are imperfect sources at best, your style is imperfect to some degree. So even when you decide to resolve the conflict, your approach may not be as effective as you would hope.

Just what is your style? The following exercise will help you identify your particular style for resolving conflict with your spouse. Complete the exercise with your spouse in mind. If you wish, you can repeat the exercise with another relationship in mind, such as a child or parent. You may find that your conflict-resolution style is different with different people.

Conflict-Resolution Profile

Below you will find five boxes, each with a letter above it: *F, M, Ra, Ro,* and *D.* (See chart in figure 5.) These letters will be explained later in the chapter. In each box, circle every word that describes how you *consistently* respond to conflict with your spouse.

FIGURE 5

F

Competitive	Dominant	Purposeful
Controlling	Forceful	Strict
Decisive	Inflexible	Take-charge
Demanding	Needs to win	Values task over people
Direct	Powerful	

M

Bargainer	Motivational	Seeks favor
Compromiser	Optimistic	Seeks trade-offs
Enthusiastic	Persuasive	Smooth
Impulsive	Promoter	Values people over task
Influencer	Risk taker	

Ra

Agreeable	Loyal	Seeks acceptance
Caring	Nurturer	Sensitive
Cautious	Patient	Supportive
Desires security	Peacemaker	Values task over people
Harmonious		

Ro

Passive	Computerlike	Logical
Analytical	Critical	Predictable
Avoider	Detail oriented	Rigid
Black-white thinker	Easily frustrated	Sidestepper
	Emotionless	Values task over people

D

Compromiser	Flexible	Resolves tension
Creative	Good listener	Respectful
Diplomatic	Mediator	Seeks consensus
Explores options	Problem solver	Seeks solutions
Facilitator	Reflective	

When you have finished circling words, count the number of words you circled in the *F* box, double that number, and enter your total in the *F* space below. For example, if you circled three words in the *F* box, you would enter the number 6 in the *F* space. Repeat this procedure for the other four boxes.

F: _____ M: _____ Ra: _____ Ro: _____ D: _____

Next, plot these five numbers on the grid below. (See chart in figure 6.) For example, if you entered 14 in the *Ra* space, place a dot on the *Ra* line next to the number 14. If you entered 18 in the *D* space, place a dot on the *D* line about midway between the 14 and the 21. Continue until you have one dot on each of the vertical lines.

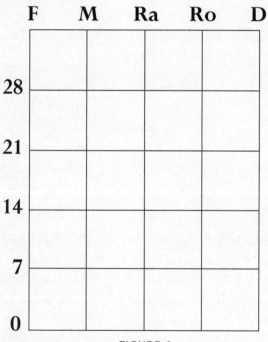

FIGURE 6

Now connect the dots to create a graph: your conflict-resolution profile. The highest peak on your graph indicates your predominant style of conflict resolution. The second highest peak suggests your second most predominant style, and so on. In order to interpret these five styles, Barb is going to use a popular syndicated TV program to introduce five common styles for conflict resolution.

FIVE COMMON CONFLICT-RESOLUTION STYLES

Gary and I love to come home from our daily radio program, cook up a great dinner, and then sit back and watch *Everybody Loves Raymond*. While we don't recommend this program for children, we believe the five main characters on this program represent five different ways people deal with conflict. Conflict is usually not a happy subject, but we find ourselves laughing at the ways these characters relate when the sparks fly in their family.

Almost every episode of *Everybody Loves Raymond* focuses on conflict. Marie, Raymond's mother, is always trying to get her way by manipulating the rest of the family. Frank, Raymond's father, is usually grousing and bellowing, trying to keep Marie under control.

Raymond, their son and the show's star, invariably tries to keep peace in the family. Torn between his loyalty and love for his parents and trying to convince his wife, Debra, that he truly can stand up to his family, Raymond is constantly in turmoil.

Raymond's older brother, Robert, vacillates between trying to upstage Raymond, the favored son, and doing anything just to keep peace, even if it means giving in to others' wishes. Sometimes he's just thankful that he isn't Raymond, caught in the middle of the family. At other times he wishes he received the attention Raymond does.

Each of these fictional characters represents a different style of conflict resolution. They correspond to the first four letters on your conflict-resolution profile: *F* is for Frank, *M* is for Marie, *Ra* is for Raymond, and *Ro* is for Robert. We will consider the *D* style later in the chapter.

The Frank Style: Win

One of Frank's most familiar lines is, "Marie, get me a sandwich." He loves to throw out one-liners, invariably frustrated with Marie and all the nonsense his wife and sons get into. He sputters, fusses, and fumes, trying to show Marie that he's the boss and trying to get his way. And it even works—sometimes.

The people who use this style go into a marital conflict with one thing in mind: winning. They have a high need to control people and situations. The idea is to pull out all the stops and control others, making sure everything and everybody goes their way. This is not the healthiest way to heal hurt and anger in a marriage. These people rarely put much emphasis on the relationship itself because they are too focused on the issue at hand and making sure they don't get the short end of the stick.

Is the win style ever preferable? Yes, it works well in difficult situations when someone needs to take charge and get a job done quickly. At times you don't have the luxury of getting input from others, even though such decisions may be met with real resistance.

The Marie Style: Persuade

"Oh, Raymond, would you like something to eat? I know Debra can't cook, and that's why you come over all the time. And while you're here, you know she really is off base in the way she handles my grandchildren." Can't you just hear Marie's lilting, cajoling voice? Marie knows just how to raise an eyebrow, pit Raymond against Debra, play to whichever son is in her favor at the time, and even throw a zinger at Frank when she gets the opportunity. She is a master of persuasion, sweet-talking her husband one minute and then giving him a one-two punch the next to get what she wants.

Marie represents another less-than-healthy conflict-resolution style in a marriage. Persuaders are often manipulative, working every angle to gain the advantage. They also have a high need to control their spouses. On the plus side, persuaders are more relational in the midst of a conflict, reasoning instead of dominating people and pushing them away—as Frank's style does. By manipulating people, persuaders may get their way in the short run, but in the long run, the persuaders' "victims" will resent them. This manipulation and ensuing resentment seriously damages the relationship.

The Raymond Style: Give In

You know Raymond, played by Ray Romano. What a great guy! Many of us relate to Raymond, feeling at times as if we just can't win. He wants to connect with his brother, Robert, but he knows Robert envies and sometimes despises him as the favored son. Raymond loves his nosy, manipulative mother and his wife, Debra, and he is always trying to keep the peace between them. And he is forever doing whatever he can to gain his father's acceptance. Raymond portrays the side in all of us that likes to keep the peace in the midst of conflict. Finding himself in the middle most of the time, he feels like he can't win.

The Raymonds are the pleasers of the world. They set aside their own needs and value the relationship above all else. They are not interested in controlling their spouses, which is healthy in most relationships. In conflict, however, they tend to give in and do what their spouses want. By consistently burying their own feelings, these people risk building up resentment below the surface. They may feel as if their spouses take advantage of them, but they can't seem to build up enough strength to take a stand.

Is this style ever useful? Of course, especially when you don't place much value on the results. We need to choose our battles carefully, realizing that sometimes the relationship is more important than the issue.

The Robert Style: Avoid

Robert, Raymond's brother, always wants everyone to settle down and relax. He would probably describe Frank as hotheaded, Marie as stirring things up, and Raymond as giving in to everybody. But Robert would rather just sit down, have a sandwich and a piece of cake (which was probably prepared for Raymond), and enjoy having a nice, quiet evening with no hassles. However, with the powerful personalities of Frank and Marie, Robert seldom enjoys a peaceful life.

The Robert style prefers to avoid conflict in marriage and family relationships. A nap sounds like a safer way to deal with interpersonal difficulties. So when conflict rears its ugly head, avoiding spouses may leave the room, clam up, change the subject, or shut down emotionally. They have a low need to control. However, total avoidance is unhealthy because it places such a low priority on the relationship.

Is there any benefit to avoidance? Yes, especially if you are dealing with a powerful personality. If a Frank-type is trying to overpower you, "pulling a Robert" can buy you some time to think things through. But you must be willing to step up to the plate at some point and resolve the conflict, resisting the inertia that sometimes accompanies avoidance. Unfortunately, many avoiders never do get back in the game. Withdrawing from conflict as a pattern can develop a hardened heart, and conflicts can remain buried for years.

If you take a closer look at these four styles, you will see that they all have drawbacks. (See the chart in figure 7.) Notice that:

The *win style* places high priority on control but a low priority on the relationship. This person is likely to ride roughshod over his or her spouse in a conflict.

The *persuade style* gives high priority to the relationship but also scores high in the need to control. This spouse will use charm and manipulation to get what he or she wants in a conflict.

The *give-in style* highly values the relationship but places low priority on control. In conflict, this person will usually cave in to his or her spouse, becoming a doormat.

The *avoid style* ranks both the relationship and control on the low end. This spouse is always looking for a way to avoid dealing with marital conflict.

FIGURE 7

The Debra Style: Resolve

We have purposely left out one of the main characters to this point. Raymond's wife, Debra, exemplifies the most effective approach to conflict in relationships: work toward resolution. Debra isn't perfect. At times she gives in to Marie's zingers just as Raymond does. After all, she's only human, and when her mother-in-law consistently tries to control her, Debra occasionally caves in. And yet, most of the time Debra is in the middle of things, trying to resolve the conflicts sparking around her.

Debra tries to cut through all the games by striving for directness and honesty in the family. She usually knows how to resolve conflicts between the various relationships. When Raymond and Robert are returning to their adolescent ways, she will step up and in her steady, mature manner, assert how important it is to value the relationship while confronting the issue. Even when Marie pushes all Debra's buttons, she can—sometimes reluctantly—move close to Marie and win her back, helping her to see the big picture. Even Frank, the crotchety curmudgeon, can be won over by Debra.

Debra exercises just the right balance between a healthy need to control and a healthy priority on relationships. She doesn't try to win or avoid. She doesn't persuade or give in. She tends to hit the issues head-on in an endearing way that often opens the door to conflict resolution and a happy ending. In part 3 of this book, Gary and I will coach you on a strategy for resolving conflicts and healing hurts in your marriage—a strategy that would make Debra proud.

When you look back over the conflicts you have experienced in your marriage, which style have you employed most of the time? Does it match the results of your conflict-resolution profile in this chapter? If you are like most people, you haven't always dealt with your marital conflicts in the healthiest manner.

You've probably reached many forks in the road during conflicts with your spouse. You probably have a good idea which road you should take, yet you have difficulty starting to move in the right direction. You face several hindrances to taking positive, healing steps in a conflict situation. Gary and I refer to these as "red lights" at the fork in the road. We will discuss them in the next chapter.

Red Lights on the Road to Healing

You walk in the door after a long day. Instead of greeting you warmly as usual, your spouse is cool and distant. Something is wrong between you, and you have an idea what it might be. There was an exchange of words and a minor clash of opinions at breakfast. You both had to leave for work before you could talk it out. In the busyness of the day, you forgot about the exchange. But now you are clearly aware that your partner hasn't forgotten.

You know you should bring the issue out into the open and get it resolved. But you don't take the initiative, and neither does your spouse. Instead, the two of you talk about surface stuff over dinner with the kids and stay busy enough at other projects through the evening not to talk at all. Even the bedtime kiss is cooler than usual.

You lie awake in the dark because your insides are churning. You hate it when there is something hanging in the air between you. Even worse, you hate yourself for not doing anything about it. Why didn't you do something?

Barb and I are convinced that sometimes we all fail to do the right thing when we come to the fork in the road for resolving conflict. Instead of moving forward and resolving the problem quickly, biblically, and peacefully, we either attempt to resolve it our own way or withdraw and let it go unresolved. It's as if there is a big red light standing in the middle of the road to resolution.

It freezes us in our tracks or prompts us to veer onto an alternate, less-effective route. We know we need to work on the conflict, but something seems to hold us back.

Recognizing and overcoming these emotional red lights is another critical step to exercising forgiving love and divorce-proofing your marriage. Barb and I will consider several of them in this chapter.

RED LIGHT 1: PRIDE

Pride may be the most destructive and harmful impediment to healing in a marriage. As the Bible tells us, "Pride goes before destruction, and haughtiness before a fall" (Proverbs 16:18).

The kind of pride we're talking about is not the warm feeling of pride we have in our family, our work, or our country. We're talking about the kind of pride that says, "I run my own life, and I don't want any interference from others." It's the pride that refuses to admit faults, placing all the blame for problems and conflicts on others. It's the pride that causes a husband and wife to hunker down in their respective trenches and refuse to make the first step toward peace.

Harold had been frozen by the red light of pride for a number of years. At age fifty-seven, he had succeeded in virtually every area of his life. In business he was a corporate vice-president with an income approaching seven figures. He had been president of his service club for three terms, and the group had raised more money for charity with each succeeding term. As an antique car enthusiast, Harold had restored several prize-winning classic cars. On top of it all, he was renowned as a gourmet chef when he and his wife, Desiree, hosted dinner parties for their many friends.

The one area in which Harold was failing instead of succeeding was a big one: his marriage. Fourteen years earlier, their twenty-two-year-old son, Jake, took his own life with a massive drug overdose. Harold and Desiree were devastated and broken. Then, soon after the funeral, Harold started the accusations with his wife: "If you had only trained him better as a boy, Desiree, this might not have happened. You should have controlled his behavior as a teenager. He wouldn't have fallen in with the wrong crowd if you had been on top of things."

Desiree was crushed, not only by Harold's harsh and persistent blame but also by his unwillingness to shoulder any of the responsibility. He would not admit that his extensive business travel and fanatical devotion to his hobbies and projects might have contributed to Jake's problems. As a result, the couple was popular and well liked by many, but they were strangers to each other behind closed doors.

To Harold, admitting that there is a conflict, let alone admitting that he may be at least partially responsible for it, is a weakness. His pride is pushing his marriage to the brink of divorce.

The antithesis of pride is humility. C. S. Lewis wrote in *Mere Christianity*, "If anyone would like to acquire humility, I can, I think, tell him the first step. The first step is to realise that one is proud. And a biggish step, too. At least, nothing whatever can be done before it."[1] It is a "biggish step" to admit our pride, but it is the only way to turn that red light to green and get on with healing.

Exercising humility allows the Harolds of the world to stand back and take a long look inside. We see where we lack forgiving love in our marriages and how to close the open loops of conflict. Humility is a gift we rarely ask for because it usually comes in the form of some difficult lessons. But it is indeed a gift.

RED LIGHT 2: GUILT

Mark's head hung so low it looked as if he might never raise his eyes again. "I really did it this time, Gary," he said, "and I can't go back."

Mark worked as a comptroller in a manufacturing plant. He met Mary at the small Christian college they both attended, and they married soon after graduation. Mary came from a wealthy background, while Mark grew up in a working-class home and was the first in his family to attend college. They were both forty-three years old when Mark came to see me. The couple had one child in college and another in high school.

Mary enjoyed having nice things, and Mark tried to meet her desires. Though they were on a modest budget, he kept encouraging her to buy what she wanted. Mark was determined to provide for his wife the way other men in their circle of friends did, so he kept using credit cards and delaying payments. He felt terrible about the big financial hole he had plunged them into, but he couldn't bring himself to tell Mary about it.

Then one day, Mark made a decision that would change the course of their lives forever. He discovered a $12,000 error in the company's books. Sitting at his desk reviewing the figures, he congratulated himself on a job well done. But then a dark thought took him by surprise: *What if I didn't tell anyone about the error? Nobody else would be able to find it. The $12,000 is there for the taking.*

He knew it was wrong, but then he thought about all the raises he had been promised but had never been given. *No one is looking out for me here,* he thought. *And trying to keep up with Mary's spending is getting harder all the time. Maybe I can just take the money for a couple of months and then pay it back later. No one will ever know.*

Can you see the web of rationalizations? Mark gave in to the temptation and never returned the money as he had planned. Now he was in my office because his actions were about to be revealed by a company audit.

Mark's inability to be honest with Mary about their finances helped create his problem in the first place. But after he committed the crime, he began living with guilt. As that guilt weighed on him, he became more moody and irritable, harder to get along with. Mary knew something was wrong but didn't know what it was. Mark avoided any conflict over family finances because he did not want to admit his crime.

Mark was filled with self-condemnation and feelings of failure as he sat in my office. "What will Mary say? How will I ever face my kids and my parents? How will I support my family? What will happen if I go to prison?" Guilt had blocked Mark from resolving his conflict with Mary and his secrecy only allowed things to get worse. He would be dealing with the consequences of his actions for many years.

The good news about guilt is that it can lead us to a loving relationship with God. The apostle Paul wrote: "God can use sorrow in our lives to help us turn away from sin and seek salvation. We will never regret that kind of sorrow. But sorrow without repentance is the kind that results in death" (2 Corinthians 7:10).

The red light of unresolved guilt can inhibit the restoration of a broken relationship. When you feel guilty, you need to ask yourself a pointed question: Have I violated a law of God or humanity that would lead me to feel what I'm feeling? If you must answer yes, perhaps your guilt is constructive and can lead you to repentance and healing. Confronting guilt and repenting is a difficult step, but the freedom you experience is so much more refreshing than the terrible burden you feel when you do not face up to it.

RED LIGHT 3: LAZINESS

Laziness is a subtle but dangerous enemy of closing loops, a glaring red light for many couples in conflict. When people are single, they often don't realize how much work a marriage relationship requires. The big task is finding and courting a potential spouse. Once the chase is over and they have said "I do," they kick into neutral, intending to coast through the marriage. They put a lot of effort into courtship, but they are not willing to put in the grunt work of making that marriage relationship last a lifetime. When conflict arises, they are too lazy to deal with it. They pull away from the heat and escape into their fantasies with activities such as hobbies, television, shopping, or sports. Hurt and anger go unhealed when laziness blocks a husband or wife from working through the conflicts they face.

John and Deb have been struggling for years over John's apparent lack of interest in dealing with conflicts in their family. When John returns home from work, he immediately turns on the television. There he sits for hours on end, night after night, watching sitcoms and sporting events. It drives Deb nuts.

Deb grew up in an active family that was always working in the yard, playing sports, or participating in family activities together. During their courting years, John spent lots of time with Deb, and he was creative in planning special times together. But during the last few years, he has nearly removed himself from any real family activity, and it hurts Deb deeply. And whenever Deb tries to talk to John about it, he is too absorbed in the TV to listen and respond. Their love has grown cold and they have drifted into the perilous waters of emotional divorce.

Laziness can kill a marriage. It indicates apathy, and apathetic people are never willing to put the time and effort into making a marriage work. At the end of their lives, they look back and realize they forfeited the intimacy and love they really wanted in marriage. Laziness leads to regret, remorse, pain, and divorce.

RED LIGHT 4: SHAME

Annie ran from my office, tears rolling down her cheeks. Her husband, Scott, looked at me in bewilderment. "Every time we start talking about what's going on, she cries," Scott said. "I don't know how to respond."

Here was a couple trying to develop their marriage in a

healthy way. But a voice kept echoing in Annie's ears from her childhood, the voice of her mother: "Can't you ever clean this kitchen the way I told you to?"; "That boy touched you again, didn't he? I told you to stay away from him. That's all he wants"; "I don't know what I'm going to do with you. Just look at you! You're filthy, and Grandma is coming this afternoon. Can't I leave you alone for one minute?"

Annie grew up with messages of shame delivered by a mother who probably had grown up in the same type of supercritical home environment. As an adult, Annie heard those messages constantly in her mind whenever she and Scott faced a conflict. Those messages came out with the same tone of shame, and always with tears: "I will never do it right, Scott. I know I'll come up short in your eyes"; "I can't go to the party looking like this. Go on without me. I'll never be ready on time"; "It's no use. I'll never change."

Scott hurt for his wife. They both wanted to learn how to deal with their conflicts. But every time they began talking about a problem between them, Annie would shut down or become overly defensive, and Scott would throw up his hands in disgust and frustration. They were rarely able to resolve a conflict because Annie's feelings of shame continually blocked the process.

Annie's deep sense of inferiority stemmed from a history of coming up short, first in the eyes of her parents and then in her own eyes. At times, shame pulled Annie into a shell of withdrawal and isolation, and she didn't want anyone around her. At other times, she felt driven to try to measure up to an elusive set of standards that were beyond her reach. This combination of humiliation, self-loathing, perfectionism, defensiveness, and uncertainty about herself had poisoned Annie's heart and was ruining their marriage.

Shame can also be the result of painful childhood or adolescent experiences, such as sexual or physical abuse. The pain from these past conflicts is so great that the victims are unwilling or seemingly unable to talk about them. We have counseled many people who have suffered unspeakable abuse in the past but have never told their spouses about it. So they carry the shameful secret around, praying it never surfaces to disturb the thin veneer covering their pain. In the meantime, they avoid dealing with conflict for fear that it will expose their shame.

How does the red light of shame differ from the red light of guilt? Guilt relates to behavior; people feel guilty for what they *did*. Shame relates to the individual; people feel shame for who they *are*. In her excellent book, *Released From Shame*, Sandra Wilson wrote, "Shame is a sense of being uniquely and hopelessly flawed. Shame leaves a person feeling different from and less valuable than other human beings."[2]

People whose lives are shadowed by shame usually try to cope in two ways, both of them counterproductive to resolving conflict. First, they may strive for perfection in their lives, hoping it will earn them the attention and approval they lacked in childhood. But perfectionists resist confessing faults and seeking forgiveness, which are vital to healing hurts.

Second, they may strive for control in their relationships and activities, assuming that being in charge will make their lives more predictable and safe, and thus less painful. But a mind-set of control often blocks people from conceding their offenses, making attempts at conflict resolution one-sided and ineffective.

The shame-controlled person needs to understand and internalize two key biblical concepts. The first is grace. When the apostle Paul cried out to God to remove his weaknesses, God's answer was to trust in his grace. Paul wrote, "But [God] said to me, 'My grace is sufficient for you, for my power is made perfect in weakness.' Therefore I will boast all the more gladly about my weaknesses, so that Christ's power may rest on me" (2 Corinthians 12:9, NIV). It is in our very weakness that God will display his power in our lives—if we let him.

The second key concept is regeneration. Shame-filled people must release their negative view of themselves and embrace their true identity as the people God made them to be when they placed their faith in Jesus Christ. The apostle Paul wrote to the church at Ephesus: "Throw off your old evil nature and your former way of life, which is rotten through and through, full of lust and deception. Instead, there must be a spiritual renewal of your thoughts and attitudes. You must display a new nature because you are a new person, created in God's likeness—righteous, holy, and true" (Ephesians 4:22-24).

Receiving God's gift of new life allows us to release to him once and for all the sins of our past. We may not completely forget them, but thanks to God's grace and forgiveness we can move past them and find a healthy way of resolving marital conflicts.

The fifth red light may be the most formidable of all. Barb will describe the role fear plays in blocking us from healing the hurts in our marriages.

RED LIGHT 5: FEAR

All of us fear something, such as air travel, snakes, spiders, or heights. I must admit that I'm afraid of fire. When I was seven years old, I returned from a school field trip to find fire trucks in front of our house. To my horror, the garage had burned to the ground, killing my beloved English setter, Bully, who had been trapped inside. Even after all these years, this memory brings a lump to my throat. I am still often very tentative around fire. At times the sound of sirens or the smell of smoke will tap into this childhood fear.

Most of these kinds of fears are not debilitating in our lives, and some of them are even laughable. But some fears can block us from resolving conflicts in our marriages.

Fear is primarily a response to something that we perceive as overpowering or threatening in our lives. Fear can exert either a positive or a negative force on us. In the Bible, we are instructed to fear God, meaning that we are to respect and defer to his power in our lives. A healthy fear of God is manifested in our trust in God. Ironically, a respectful, trusting fear of God can help deliver us from other fears that can damage our lives and marriages. In other words, the more we fear God in the proper sense of the term, the less we will fear those things that keep us from being the persons and spouses we want to be.

The apostle Paul knew about fear in the face of conflict. He stated, "When we arrived in Macedonia there was no rest for us. Outside there was conflict from every direction, and inside there was fear" (2 Corinthians 7:5). For many of us, that's how we live life. We struggle through the conflicts in our marriages and feel a dread and fear within. Many people know they need to resolve certain conflicts, and often they know how to go about it. But they are afraid. They lack the courage to confront a real or perceived threat. So they avoid dealing with the issue, deciding instead to play it safe. Here are four fears that prevent people from resolving conflict.

Fear of Failure

For years Beth had known that her husband's eating habits were contributing to his poor health. No matter what she served him at mealtimes, Douglas ate too much. If the meal didn't satisfy him, he would top it off with a peanut-butter sandwich or two. And he was a dessert junky, especially ice cream. At forty-two, Douglas was about fifty pounds overweight, which aggravated the arthritis in his feet and hips. Beth also knew her husband was a prime candidate for heart disease. Besides the health concerns, Beth was disappointed that Douglas had so carelessly forfeited the attractive physique she had so admired when they first married.

Beth had tried to confront Douglas a number of times about his eating. She had volunteered to go on diets with him. She had encouraged him to join a gym and sign up for a personal trainer. She had suggested they see a nutritionist together. But whenever she would start in, Douglas would become upset. "You think I'm fat, and you are always hounding me about it," he would say, sounding hurt. "You don't trust me to take care of myself. If you would just quit bugging me about my eating, maybe I could do something about it."

On a few occasions, Beth actually talked Douglas into eating more sensibly at home. Then she would discover the candy bar and cupcake wrappers in his car. And at these times of supposed good behavior, Douglas was a bear to live with.

Beth is now gun shy. She is afraid this conflict will never be resolved. She has tried everything, and it hasn't worked. And the more she tries, the greater the strain on their marriage. She doesn't want to try anymore for fear that things will only get worse.

When you fear failure in your marriage, you will go to great lengths to avoid the problems and conflicts that generate your fear. Sometimes the fear of failure can become so severe that marital communication in any form is a chore. You may feel as if you don't measure up to your spouse's expectations, so you stay away physically or emotionally. By avoiding the pain of failure, you can allow conflicts to fester for years.

Fear of Success

Ironically, some people back away from conflict resolution because they are afraid of success, not failure. You may wonder, "The fear of failure makes sense, but who would be afraid of success?" People who fear success avoid taking risks because their past is so scarred by failure that success is an alien idea to them.

They stand immobile at the fork in the road because moving ahead into the unknown of healing seems more threatening than the familiarity of failure.

Subconsciously, these people reason, *If I work through and resolve this conflict with my spouse, I may have to change my behavior, and I don't know how to handle that.* Or they think, *If I clear up this conflict successfully, I'll probably mess up the next opportunity, so what's the use of trying?* Some of these people will actually sabotage conflict resolution to spare themselves the anxiety of a change in the relationship with their spouse.

Fear of Rejection

Fear of rejection is a cousin to fear of failure. It's the small voice inside that says, "If your spouse really knew what you were thinking and feeling, he or she would laugh at you and turn away from you." Fear of rejection keeps some spouses from explaining the true reasons for their conflicts. We figure that if we risk stepping out, we will be rejected again. So instead of forging ahead to resolve a conflict, we slink back into the shadows and shut down. Fear of rejection leads to a loss of self-confidence that can develop into anxiety or depression. Conflicts may persist, but the pain of discussing them is so great that avoidance seems the best route to take.

I felt deep sorrow for Penny, one of my counseling patients. Penny had been sexually abused as a child, but she never told her husband. Ed was a good husband. He provided for the family and loved their kids. But he always became angry when discussing sexual issues. He had communicated to Penny, "If anything happened before I knew you, please don't tell me. I just couldn't handle knowing about it." Penny yearned for her husband to know the truth and help her deal with the pain. But she feared that if she told Ed the truth, he might lose interest in her sexually.

We all face pressures and problems, and one of the best ways to deal with them is to talk them out with the one we love and trust the most—our spouse. Yet Penny withheld her most intimate pain from her husband. "It just isn't worth running the risk of rejection," Penny said. "I'm stuck." She was blocked from finding healing in her long-standing conflict by her fear of rejection.

Many men also harbor this fear of rejection. A husband may not discuss his sexual or emotional needs with his wife because, when he does, his wife may reject him. As a result, he may be more vulnerable to the temptation to meet his needs outside the marriage. This is how many affairs begin. If the boundaries around the marriage are not strong enough to protect it, a person may unwisely give in to the temptation of adultery.

Some people also think that if they talk honestly with their spouse about their feelings, they will be put down or rejected. They expect to hear, "You shouldn't even be thinking that, honey." But these people still may feel the need to vent their feelings to someone. Nobody wants to be judged; we just want to be heard. Honest, open, accepting communication nurtures a healthy marriage.

Fear of Emotional Intimacy

Another type of fear that can impede the resolution of conflicts in marriage is the fear of emotional intimacy. You may equate emotional intimacy with sexual intimacy, but they are very different. Many couples succeed at sexual intimacy while starving for emotional intimacy. Sexual intimacy is easy. You can come together physically and be satisfied in a short amount of time. Being close emotionally takes constant work and commitment.

People who fear emotional intimacy put up walls of protection to keep their spouses from getting close. They carefully keep their deep thoughts and feelings under wraps. They push their spouses away emotionally with angry blow-ups, or they avoid getting too close in the first place. Either way, the result is a marriage where conflicts are resolved only at the surface level and deep hurts go unhealed.

You may fear emotional intimacy because it was lacking in your family of origin. You were not close to one or both of your parents, so you never learned how to allow other people—especially your spouse—to be close to you. As such, you probably avoid dealing with conflict in order to keep the layers of self-protection intact.

This was the case with Pete and Kathy. Pete grew up in a home where chaos reigned and emotional intimacy was a myth. His father had a ferocious temper, kicking into a rage when Pete and his brothers least expected it. Looking for acceptance, Pete pulled away from his family and hung out with guys from the wrong side of the tracks. His grades dropped in high school, and like so many hurting and needy kids, he ran wild—alcohol, drugs, and sex.

In his junior year of high school, Pete met Kathy, who also came from a home lacking in emotional intimacy. These two love-starved kids tried to fill their legitimate needs for emotional intimacy through sex. Sure enough, Kathy got pregnant in their senior year and the couple got married soon after. Their early married years were marked by abuse, conflict, and emotional pain. But, amazingly, they stayed together—at least physically.

By the time they reached their thirties, Pete and Kathy were emotionally estranged. They wanted to develop a healthy relationship, but when Kathy got too close to Pete, he would shut down and withdraw, just as he did with his father. He worked long hours and hung out at the health club. Kathy was tired of trying to win Pete's heart and was beginning to distance herself from him. As they tried to resolve their pain, the conflicts only intensified. They found it all too easy to slip back into the hurtful patterns of their upbringing. Living in an emotional desert was gradually killing the joy in their marriage and damaging their relationship with their son.

When Gary met with Pete and Kathy, they were ready to throw in the towel. "Dr. Rosberg, it's too late for us," they lamented. But it wasn't too late. They needed to establish healthy patterns of communication, and they also needed someone to model a strong marriage for them.

Gary learned that Pete had a deep-seated fear of emotional intimacy. He felt that if he became too vulnerable, Kathy would leave him. As Pete learned new strategies for getting close to his wife, the two of them developed a greater sense of trust. Eventually the walls of self-protection came down as their emotional intimacy grew. Pete took the risk of letting Kathy into his life. He cut down his hours at work and they started working out at the club together. As their emotional intimacy grew, their marriage improved.

Pete now realizes that his fear of emotional intimacy was caused by the hurt he experienced as a child. Now he no longer sees Kathy as the villain. He can trust her with his heart, and Kathy cherishes the closeness they are now experiencing.

Slaying the Dragons of Fear

Here is a vivid image that will help you deal with any fears that may be blocking you from the path of conflict resolution and healing. Someone shared this picture with Gary and me several years ago, and we have used it in our own personal lives and in our counseling ever since.

If some kind of fear is standing between you and the healing you desire in your marriage, picture that fear as a fierce, fire-breathing dragon. Every time you even think of taking a step in the right direction, that dragon roars and breathes fire at you, keeping you at bay. The more you feed that fear with irrational thinking and worry, the more the dragon grows. The only way to stop the growth and move ahead is to slay the dragon.

How do you slay the dragon of fear? By confronting it with the truth. Fear is mentioned hundreds of times in the Bible. But more than three hundred times we are told by our all-knowing heavenly Father to "fear not." Paul wrote to Timothy, "God has not given us a spirit of fear and timidity, but of power, love, and self-discipline" (2 Timothy 1:7). Our fears may seem invincible, but they are no match for the power, love, and self-discipline we have from the indwelling Holy Spirit.

Whether you struggle with the fear of failure, success, rejection, or emotional intimacy (any or all of them), you can defeat your fears by demonstrating faith in the God who empowers us to slay all our dragons.

RED LIGHT 6: CONTROL

The issue of control centers on the struggle for dominance or power in the marriage relationship. Gary and I often use the TV remote-control device (like some of you, we simply call it the "clicker") as a symbol of control in the home. The person who holds the clicker holds the power over the television—whether it's on or off and what programs are on the screen.

One night Gary and I were lying in bed watching TV. It happened to be a program I had selected. But as so often happens, Gary confiscated the clicker and started flipping through the channels "just to see what else is on." But as he channel-flipped, the TV kept coming back to the station I selected. He was mystified. "What is wrong with this dumb TV?" he muttered. I couldn't control my giggles. Finally Gary discovered the *other* clicker, the one I had secretly purchased and hidden on my side of the bed just to give him a hard time. I had been outdueling him for control of the channels and he didn't even know it! We've had some good laughs over that one.

There are two kinds of controllers: active and passive. Active controllers want to call the shots, make the decisions, determine the course of action, and otherwise dominate what happens in their relationships. Active controllers often block healthy conflict resolution by not regarding a spouse's opinions, needs, or suggestions. Or if both partners happen to be active controllers, they will spend their time arguing and seldom reach a resolution.

Passive controllers have a low need for control and a high need to please. When it comes to conflict, they also have opinions, needs, and suggestions, but they will often back off to keep the peace and make their spouse happy. Or they will simply walk away and avoid the conflict. Passive controllers can block conflict resolution just as effectively as active controllers. By allowing their partner to dominate, often their needs in the conflict are unstated and thus unmet, so the conflict continues to simmer beneath the surface.

What's the biblical response to the problem of active or passive control in marital conflicts? I think there is a helpful picture in Revelation 3:20, where Jesus says: "Look! Here I stand at the door and knock. If you hear me calling and open the door, I will come in, and we will share a meal as friends." Jesus is a gentleman. He doesn't bust down the door of your marriage and take over like an active controller. Nor does he stand timidly at the door unnoticed like a passive controller. Rather, he knocks and politely waits to be invited in.

You disarm the threat of control in marriage conflicts the same way. Active controllers, you must learn to back off and knock, as it were, instead of running roughshod over conflict resolution by asserting dominance. Extend your partner the courtesy of asking his or her opinions, learning his or her needs, and hearing his or her suggestions. Passive controllers, instead of always being the doormat, you need to find the courage to step up to the door and knock. Learn to express yourself respectfully but unequivocally. The more you emulate Jesus' courteous example in your relationship, the easier it will be to deal with your conflicts and find healing.

I would like to leave you with one other picture that will help with the issue of control and all the other red lights we have discussed in this chapter. Imagine that you are driving your car down a deserted road one dark, foggy night. You haven't seen another car for miles. Then suddenly your headlights illuminate a figure standing beside the road. As you draw closer, you are amazed to see that it's Jesus, and he has his thumb out, hoping to hitch a ride.

You don't normally pick up hitchhikers, but you know you can trust Jesus. So you slow the car and invite him to slip into the backseat. But he just stands there. You quickly realize that he probably prefers riding in front, so your spouse hops out and gets into the backseat, leaving the front passenger door open for Jesus. Still the Savior doesn't move.

After several silent moments, Jesus finally walks around to your side of the car and taps on your window. You roll it down quickly, and Jesus says only two words: "Move over."

Jesus didn't come to be a passenger in our lives or our marriages. He is forgiving love personified, and he came to drive. He came to be in charge. He alone knows how to get you through the red lights that have immobilized you in your attempts to resolve your conflicts. But, ever the gentleman, he will not barge in and take control. He patiently knocks and waits for us to give him control of ourselves and our marriage relationships.

Nonnegotiables for Closing the Loop

Barb and I were recently out with some friends whose twenty-something daughter was getting a divorce from her husband. Seven years of marriage, a three-year-old daughter, their whole lives before them, and they have walked away from it all. It's breaking the hearts of everyone who knows them. Individually, this husband and wife are wonderful people. But they just can't figure out how to resolve conflict, so they have chucked it all in hopes of finding their perfect soul mates elsewhere.

As we sat gazing into the eyes and souls of our dear friends, I remembered a talk I had with a buddy of mine several years earlier. I had sought his counsel regarding another relationship on the verge of a breakup.

"Do you have a minute, Stu?"

"Sure, Gary. Let's grab a sandwich. What's up?"

Stu Weber and I have been friends for a number of years. He's the pastor of a large church near Portland, Oregon, and the author of the classic book for men, *Tender Warrior*. On this particular day, Stu and I were speaking at a conference in Minneapolis. I was really hurting, and I needed to talk to someone. So, during a break in the conference, Stu and I got away for lunch together.

"Stu, Barb and I are in the middle of one of the most difficult experiences in our lives," I began. "We are very close to a couple who is going through an immense amount of pain. We've known these people and admired them deeply for almost twenty years, since we were in college together. Theirs was the kind of marriage we wanted to model ours after. But over the last couple of years, they have been tremendously stressed. Their marriage is being torn apart, Stu, and it's breaking our hearts."

"Have you talked to them about your concern?" Stu asked.

"Yes, we have. But we're frustrated because we're so close to both of them that we can't keep a sense of clarity about the issues. I think we're too numbed by our own pain to deal with this. We don't know what to do. It feels like we are going through a divorce ourselves. We have never felt as helpless in counseling someone as we do right now."

Stu's response was direct, simple, and profound. "Gary, in my dearest relationships—with my wife, Lindy, my three sons, and my church—I have determined that nothing is more important than the relationship itself. These relationships are nonnegotiable. Anything else, other than the Bible, is open for discussion. But I am committed to these relationships—period."

I sat in that deli looking into the eyes of a man who once led troops in Vietnam as a Green Beret. That day he led me into a clearer understanding of a problem that had been weighing on our hearts for months. What we needed to do was love this man and woman unconditionally and realize that our relationship with each of them was nonnegotiable. No matter what happened, we would maintain our relationship with them. We didn't have to agree with what they were doing, we didn't have to take sides, and we sure didn't have to fix their problem. We simply needed to let them know that they meant more to us than the problem at hand. The issues dividing them were negotiable and up for discussion, but our commitment to them personally was not.

And that's just what Barb and I did. We just wish our friends had adopted the same attitude toward each other. While we remain close to these two people individually, they ended their marriage in divorce.

As we prepare to walk you through six vital steps for closing the loops of conflict in your lives in part 3, we want to challenge you to adopt a few nonnegotiables in your relationship. Consider them the ground rules or boundaries for forgiving love in your marriage. Each of them is a line in the sand, something you each determine not to cross under any circumstances. These nonnegotiables are indispensable for divorce-proofing your marriage.

NONNEGOTIABLE 1: DIVORCE IS NOT AN OPTION

The first nonnegotiable we challenge you to embrace is this: No matter how bad the conflict and pain may be, you must be committed to stay together and work it out. Divorce is not an option. As you stand at the fork in the road concerning the conflicts you face, your choices really boil down to this: Are you going to let this conflict go unresolved, allowing your heart to grow hard, or are you going to move ahead by faith no matter what stands in your way and do whatever it takes to resolve this conflict? In other words, will you choose to lovingly rebuild the relationship or run the risk that your marriage will end up on the rocks? Your total commitment to each other and to your marriage is the most critical factor to closing the loop.

Many individuals and couples we talk to view marriage as a gamble, a roll of the dice. They go into it hoping it will work out, but if it doesn't, divorce is always a way to bail out. Because this idea is so prevalent in our culture, when I take two young people through premarital counseling, I urge them to consider their marriage to be an unbreakable vow. They need to commit themselves unconditionally to each other. They need to declare, "Divorce is not an option for us."

You need to view your marriage as a covenant, not a contract. A contract focuses on what you will *get* out of the relationship. A covenant focuses on what you will *give* to the relationship. In a covenant marriage, divorce is not an option.

Resolving marital conflicts is a lot like trapeze work. You have to take some risks, you may experience a little—or more than a little—fear or anxiety, and you always face the danger of failing. The trapeze artists and high-wire acrobats at the circus can take great risks because they know there is a net there to catch them. Without the net, they may limit their stunts because of their fear of falling.

The nonnegotiable of total commitment to the relationship is like a safety net. When there is a net to catch you, you may be willing to take greater risks and look past the fear. When dealing with the difficult issues, you can go for it without fear because the marriage is never in jeopardy. Your spouse is not going to leave you no matter what the outcome, and you are not going to leave your spouse. The decision to stay together has already been made. It is nonnegotiable.

A no-divorce commitment will not prevent you from experiencing conflict. But it will compel you to resolve those conflicts because you are committed to staying together. The more secure you are in your relationship, the better prepared you are to work through your conflicts.

NONNEGOTIABLE 2: MY SPOUSE IS NOT MY ENEMY

When Barb and I speak at the Weekend to Remember conferences, we instruct couples to look each other in the eye and repeat a statement that we hope will burn into their consciousness: "My spouse is not my enemy." We love that message! So often in the midst of a conflict, husband and wife fire poison darts directly at each other's hearts. They see each other as deadly adversaries. But the essential truth is that you are on the same team. You need to work together to restore your family to wholeness, to defeat the isolation you have experienced. Since you are not enemies, you will reject the easier option of avoiding or caving in to conflict and will team up to resolve it.

When you realize that you are not enemies, the issues that divide you are subjected to the relationship that unites you. The conflict still brings hurt and anger, but you choose to face the issues, express your needs, listen to each other, and restore the relationship. The truly nonnegotiable relationship always finds a way to become vital once again.

The pain you feel after an offense may prompt you to shut down and walk away from your spouse. But you can also allow it to become a stimulus to reach out to someone more powerful than yourself—someone who is always available to you, someone who really understands the pain and your desire to pull away. That someone, of course, is Jesus.

God sometimes uses the pain in our lives to get our attention. As C. S. Lewis put it in *The Problem of Pain*, "God whispers to us in our pleasures, speaks in our conscience, but shouts in our pains: it is his megaphone to rouse a deaf world."[1] The apostle Paul said it even better in Romans 5: "We can rejoice, too, when we run into problems and trials, for we know that they are good for us—they help us learn to endure. And endurance develops strength of character in us, and character strengthens our confident expectation of salvation" (Romans 5:3-4).

Once you decide that your relationship is nonnegotiable, you still need the strength to take the first step toward closing the loop. That's why it is so important to recognize how God can use your pain. If you allow it to direct you to God, he will give you the strength and power to resolve the conflict.

NONNEGOTIABLE 3:
GOD'S WAY IS ALWAYS BEST

Closing the loop takes more than just skill and effort. It requires that we utilize timeless biblical principles to bring new life to a lethargic relationship. Specifically, it takes three ingredients that, when applied together, create a richness in the restoration of a broken relationship.

Obedience

Jack and Charlene's marriage had been bad for a long time, but it finally hit the wall during their eleventh year. They argued constantly and felt no love for each other. As Christians, they knew divorce was wrong, but they just couldn't stand living together anymore. Eventually Jack moved out, and as they contemplated ending the marriage, both Jack and Charlene got emotionally involved with other people.

Gene, their pastor and long-time friend, lovingly confronted them one day. He said, "I know you two don't feel like being married. But I challenge you to stay together and work it out anyway."

"Give us one good reason why we should, Gene," they argued.

Gene looked them squarely in the eyes. "Because that's what God wants you to do. And if you obey God, he will rekindle your love for each other."

The couple didn't like Gene's answer, but they couldn't refute it. Reluctantly, they agreed to accept Gene's challenge. They decided to speak to each other civilly and do the right thing by each other. It was tough at first because they still despised each other. They were merely gritting it through because it was the right thing to do. And when one of them failed to do the right thing, the other was quick to condemn or criticize.

During subsequent talks with Gene, Jack and Charlene

learned to let go of controlling the other and do what God was calling each of them to do as individuals. As they followed this counsel, they began to realize that as they obeyed God instead of trying to control or correct each other, their relationship began to change for the better. Over the following months and years, God did restore their love.

Jack and Charlene's discovery parallels the findings of a research study conducted by Linda J. Waite, professor of sociology at the University of Chicago. The study revealed that "86 percent of those who rated their marriage as unhappy in the late 80s and who were still married five years later said their marriages had become happier."[2] Just staying together is what some marriages need most to begin healing.

Today, as Jack and Charlene approach their thirtieth anniversary, they are more in love than they ever thought they could be. They are so glad they committed to obey God despite their negative feelings toward each other. God has used Jack and Charlene to minister to countless numbers of Christian couples whose marriages were on the rocks. Their advice is simple: "Obey God even when you don't feel like it, and he will rekindle your love for each other."

The apostle Paul challenged the Christians at Corinth, "The reason I wrote you was to see if you would stand the test and be obedient in everything" (2 Corinthians 2:9, NIV). Do you ever feel as if you are being tested in your marriage? Do you sometimes wonder if it's worth the hassle to do the right thing? Every difficulty and conflict is a kind of test. Will you stand the test and remain obedient in everything?

Throughout the Bible, the truly great men and women obeyed God implicitly and immediately, despite the circumstances. Abraham pulled up stakes and moved when God said move, even though he didn't know where he would end up. He also was ready to sacrifice his son Isaac on the altar at God's command.

Moses took on the task of leading the Jews out of Egypt even though he didn't feel qualified. The disciples left their homes and businesses to obey Christ's call to follow him.

Just as the men and women of the Bible were called to be obedient, so are we as husbands and wives. We are called to close open loops of conflict and let God heal our hurts. You may not always feel like it. You may not always want to. But you need to do it because it's the right thing to do. As you obey, God will work on your attitudes and emotions.

Courage

Jack and Charlene will tell you that it took courage for them to obey God and keep their marriage together. More specifically, it took real courage to face their conflicts day by day instead of retreating or giving up. They took the admonition of Psalm 27:14 to heart: "Wait patiently for the Lord. Be brave and courageous."

When you stand at the fork in the road of conflict, you need courage to do the right thing. If you hesitate to confront your spouse about an insensitive comment because you're afraid he or she will reject you, you need courage to move ahead. If you are afraid to tell your spouse about a secret sin that has brought isolation into your relationship, you need courage to be vulnerable.

God will give you the strength you need. His instructions to Joshua as the nation of Israel prepared to enter the Promised Land are applicable to the daily conflicts we must face and resolve: "Be strong and courageous, for you will lead my people to possess all the land I swore to give their ancestors. Be strong and very courageous. Obey all the laws Moses gave you. Do not turn away from them, and you will be successful in everything you do. Study this Book of the Law continually. Meditate on it day and night so you may be sure to obey all that is written in it. Only then will you succeed. I command you—be strong and courageous! Do not be afraid or discouraged. For the Lord your God is with you wherever you go" (Joshua 1:6-9).

I see two sources for our courage in this passage. First, we can proceed with confidence when we know God calls us to do something. And since we know God wants us to resolve conflicts rather than avoid them, we know we can move ahead with courage.

Second, you can proceed with confidence when you operate according to Scripture. As you will see in part 3, the Bible is full of wisdom on how to resolve conflict. You don't have to do it on your own.

Humility

Obedience and courage are insufficient for resolving conflicts without an attitude of humility. Obedience helps you meet the challenge to hang in there. Courage gives you the guts to reach out to your spouse. But humility pulls down the walls dividing you and gives you the heart of a servant to bring the tenderness back into your relationship. The apostle Paul wrote, "Don't be selfish; don't live to make a good impression on others. Be humble, thinking of others as better than yourself" (Philippians 2:3).

Humility is the capacity to put your spouse and your marriage ahead of your own wants and feelings. It's what Jesus exemplified in John 13 when he washed the feet of the disciples. You can't learn humility in a classroom; it's an element of character that must be cultivated in trials. Every time you face a conflict in your marriage and decide to fight for the good of the relationship instead of for your own personal agenda, you are exercising humility.

Barb and I have found that humility rarely comes out of the mountaintop experiences of our lives. Instead, we learn humility during those times when we slog through the middle of a storm. It's when we come to the end of ourselves, when we are broken and helpless, that God works his humility into us. That's when we are ready to admit that we don't know all the answers and turn to the one who does: Jesus Christ.

When I went through a significant bout of depression in 1996, I experienced one of those times of brokenness. I never would have wished for that experience, but the lessons I learned were invaluable. It is through brokenness that humility is forged. It is in brokenness that we learn we are not invincible or self-sufficient. It is how we discover that our relationship with Jesus and with each other as husband and wife are the most significant in our lives.

I learned one other lesson through my experience of depression. When you have been broken through tough circumstances in your life or marriage, you want to stay close to the cross of Christ and to others who are close to Christ and his sacrifice. That's where you find your strength. I have been known to say that I don't really trust a person who has not been broken. Without brokenness and humility, the temptation to go it on your own is too great.

In chapter 2, we told you the story of Dean, who had discovered that his wife, Nancy, was having an affair. When Dean told Nancy that he "knew," Nancy announced that she had already secured an apartment. Dean told me during his counseling session that he never thought he would hear such a statement come out of Nancy's mouth. And that's where we left the story. I would like to tell you what happened to this couple.

Dean had come to a major fork in the road; he had several options in this huge conflict. He could have said, "Yes, Nancy, I want you to leave. You committed adultery, you broke my heart, and it's over." Then he could have called his attorney and jumped on the fast track to divorce.

Or, instead of divorcing Nancy, Dean could have chosen to shut down emotionally, pull back, and start building a wall around his emotions. After the blow she dealt him, you can understand such responses, can't you?

But here's what actually happened. When Nancy announced that she was moving out, Dean said to her, "No, you're my wife. I want you to stay." Then he told me the rest of the story. "Stunned by my statement, Nancy tearfully confessed her affair with Tim. It had lasted a few months. Gary, I can't describe the storm of emotions that tore through me at that moment. She was so broken as she described how much she had needed me back then, yet I was too busy for her.

"It all came back to me—how often she begged me to take her out to dinner or to the movies. But I was too busy. She couldn't even lure me away from work late at night with her promises of passionate lovemaking! How could I have been so blind? This went on for many months. She would get angry with me and tell me my priorities were all messed up. But I was on a mission and would not be swayed.

"Gary, I drove my wife away! The most precious person in my life was crying out for me to meet her needs, but I wouldn't listen. Finally, she *did* find someone to listen and care: Tim."

I said to Dean, "Even in the midst of that painful encounter with Nancy, you were able to talk about the root of the conflict. That's great. What happened next?"

"I admitted to Nancy through my tears, 'I have never cheated on you physically. But I realize now that I have cheated you in another way. You reached out to me, but I was cool and distant. You kept encouraging us to connect, but I was too busy with work. I hate to admit it, but work became my mistress.' Then I wrapped her tightly in my arms, and together we cried out to God to forgive us both. I was angry at what Nancy did, and I was furious at myself for being so selfish and ignoring her needs. I had taken my heart away from God and from my wife.

"For the next several days we talked of our bitterness, anger, and fear. Some moments we found ourselves drawing close to each other, and at other moments we would pull away. I burst into tears at unpredictable moments, even when I was alone. Seeing myself in the mirror while brushing my teeth, I just started crying. I had to turn on the shower just to muffle my groans. I remember leaning over the sink with dry heaves, crying out to God.

"When my precious wife cried about how dirty she felt, we wept together about it. It was something we had never experienced before. We were in the middle of a spiritual battle over our marriage. The enemy kept whispering to us that we could never put our marriage back together again. But in God's strength, we threw those words back in the devil's face. We took a stand for our marriage, Gary. And the victory came through God's power."

It was at this fork in the road, the devastation of betrayal and infidelity, that Dean and Nancy decided that their marriage was nonnegotiable. They also realized that their relationship was not just a marriage of two; it was a marriage of three—Nancy, Dean, and God. They needed an anchor in this storm that was strong, secure, and immovable when conflicts raged. They knew God was that anchor, and they held on to him for dear life. They affirmed that God had brought them together in the first place, and only he could hold them together after what had happened.

The nonnegotiable of a divorce-proof marriage of three is a solid platform for resolving conflicts and healing hurts in your marriage. In part 3, Barb and I will coach you on specific biblical principles for closing the loop of conflict together.

PART III

THE CLOSED LOOP
OF HEALING

8

Prepare Your Heart

Finally we arrive at the most practical section of this book. Gary and I have explained how open loops of conflict bring hurt and anger into the marriage relationship. We have taken you to the fork in the road and encouraged you to step out in obedience, courage, and humility to close the loop. Now it's time to learn how to do it. What must we do to exercise forgiving love in the face of marital conflicts?

In this final section, we will explore a six-stage process for restoring a strained or broken marriage relationship: (1) prepare your heart; (2) diffuse your anger; (3) communicate your concerns; (4) confront your conflicts; (5) forgive your spouse; and (6) rebuild your trust. We will coach you through a number of practical skills at each stage of the process. We're not saying you need to march through this six-stage process legalistically with every conflict you face. But as you internalize these principles and use this process as a roadmap for resolving your conflicts, we believe you will be better equipped to respond to marital conflicts as they arise.

In this chapter, we want to talk about stage one: prepare your heart. (See the diagram in figure 8.) You may be totally sincere in your desire to resolve a conflict, but if your heart isn't right, your efforts may only make things worse. Gary and I want to share with you four steps for preparing your hearts to close the loop.

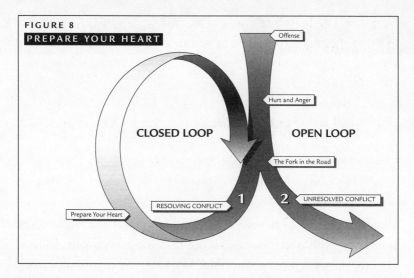

FIGURE 8

PREPARE YOUR HEART

Offense

Hurt and Anger

CLOSED LOOP　　　　**OPEN LOOP**

The Fork in the Road

RESOLVING CONFLICT　**1**　**2**　UNRESOLVED CONFLICT

Prepare Your Heart

STEP 1: TAKE A PERSONAL TIME-OUT

Have you ever said or heard someone say, "I need to get away and clear my head"? What we mean by that is isolating ourselves from the rat race of daily life for a time so we can think and plan. Even more important to healing hurts and restoring your relationship with your spouse is getting away to clear your *heart*. When there is a conflict to be dealt with, it is important to take a personal time-out for self-examination and prayer.

For you, this may mean driving to the country, the mountains, or the beach for a day—or even just for an hour or two. Your personal time-out may take the form of a walk to a nearby park or an hour spent in a quiet corner of your house. Believe me, it really doesn't matter where you go; the idea is to create some space between you and your normal routine so you can talk through your thoughts and feelings with the Lord alone and without interruption.

Sometimes when a conflict arises, you don't have time to get away. You need to deal with the issue immediately. So you are wise to schedule these occasional time-outs as a matter of course. If you never take time to allow the Lord to search your heart, you are hindering the process of conflict resolution with your spouse. In other words, if you scrimp on your time alone with God, you are hurting instead of helping your marriage relationship. Your constant prayer should be, "Search me, O God, and know my heart; test me and know my thoughts. Point out anything in me that offends you, and lead me along the path of everlasting life" (Psalm 139:23-24).

Here are four important elements to include when you take a personal time-out to clear your heart.

1. Listen to God. Open your heart during this time to what God wants to teach you. This happens best through reading the Bible. Whether I am facing a current conflict with Gary or just preparing myself for the next one to come along, I make it a point to spend time alone daily in the Word of God. I am not so much digging for a specific answer as simply allowing God to speak to me from any passage I may read. And during the process I am asking God to help me understand the truth and apply it to my life.

2. Confess your sin. Is there a violation of God's teaching you must clear up with him before you go to your spouse? Did you do or say something wrong that contributed to the conflict? Did you omit or ignore something you should have done or said? Pray along with David, "Wash me clean from my guilt. Purify me from my sin. For I recognize my shameful deeds—they haunt me day and night. Against you, and you alone, have I sinned; I have done what is evil in your sight. . . . Purify me from my sins, and I will be clean; wash me, and I will be whiter than snow" (Psalm 51:2-4, 7).

3. Talk to God in prayer. Tell him about everything—your failures, your fears, your hurts, your desire for healing. God isn't interested in flowery words; he's listening for authenticity. He already knows your heavy heart, and he longs for you to off-load your burden into his hands and trust him for resolution. He wants us to pray from the depths of our hearts. Allow the pain that you feel in your relationship to draw you into greater dependence on

God. You may pray something like this: "God, give me the understanding to be humble by resolving this issue in a way that honors you. Help me to be gracious toward my spouse and respectful of his or her perspective. Help us to talk things through. Help us to close the loop and rekindle our love for each other."

4. Determine to be a peacemaker. Jesus taught, "God blesses those who work for peace, for they will be called the children of God" (Matthew 5:9). Peacemakers please God. One of the most important aspects of resolving conflict is adopting an attitude of restoration. When we counsel couples in conflict, Gary and I can tell which spouses sincerely want to move toward healing and which ones are still looking to land a few more verbal or emotional blows. Authentic reconciliation requires two people who are committed to, and making an effort toward, peace in their marriage. If one or both spouses are not ready to work toward reconciliation, they seldom get very far in resolving their conflict.

STEP 2: LOOK FOR THE UNDERLYING CAUSES

Andrea and Rod came to Gary for counseling some time ago. They had been married for several years but were struggling with sexual intimacy in their relationship. Gary asked them several questions, trying to gain a perspective. It came out that Andrea just didn't enjoy sex, which was frustrating to Rod. But when Gary starting digging into their personal histories, both Rod and Andrea resisted the discussion. Rod said, "There wasn't any sexual abuse when we were kids, if that's what you're looking for. We just want to improve our sexual relationship today. You counselors are always snooping into the past for answers. Does it always have to be that complicated?"

Gary explained that he was simply looking for the underlying causes of their conflict, not to blame anyone but to understand in order to help. After a moment of silence, Andrea said sheepishly,

"Rod, I think we need to tell Gary about what happened before we were married." Rod agreed with reluctance, obviously defensive.

"Gary," Andrea began tentatively, "before we were married, Rod was sexually involved with another girl. I didn't know about it until our honeymoon. That's when he decided to tell me. I felt angry and betrayed. I also felt that having sex was somehow dirty. I've been confused ever since and don't know how to let go of it. I love my husband, and I want to be sexually responsive to him. But I just can't forget what he did and that he didn't tell me before we were married."

During their sessions with Gary, Rod and Andrea began to confront what Rod had been working hard to deny: the consequences of his sin. His desire to clear the air with Andrea was good, but his timing had been terrible. He not only ruined the honeymoon for Andrea but also created in her a distaste for sex, a distaste that continued through their marriage. Once Gary helped them root out the underlying cause of their conflict, they could move ahead with some genuine healing. Over time they were able to close the loop on this issue.

When you step out to resolve conflict and heal hurt, you must go deeper than the symptoms. If you are angry with your spouse, you need to know exactly where that anger is coming from. If you are hurt by something he or she said, you need to dig behind the hurt to find its root cause. Dealing only with the symptoms guarantees that the conflict will recur and probably get worse.

As we explained in previous chapters, there are many factors that can relate to our conflicts in the present, such as family training and cultural expectations. That's why developing an understanding of the past—looking at the underlying causes of our conflicts—is essential to healing. You may want to prayerfully ask yourself some of the following questions as you seek to identify the root causes of your conflict:

❧ How does my family background seem to affect the way I resolve marital conflict today? How does my spouse's family background affect how he or she resolves conflict between us?

❧ What experiences from my past may have caused the current conflict?

❧ Do I feel any root of bitterness or resentment that may be sabotaging the resolution of the current conflict? (See Hebrews 12:15.)

❧ Is there any reason I may want to maintain conflict instead of resolve it? For example, am I enjoying a measure of control over my spouse by not resolving the issue?

Looking below the surface of a conflict may be difficult and uncomfortable for you. But without an honest understanding of the underlying causes of your conflicts, the answers you find will be superficial and short-lived.

Gary is going to share with you two more vital steps in the process of preparing your heart for resolving conflicts.

STEP 3: KEEP YOUR MARRIAGE THE TOP PRIORITY

One of the greatest saboteurs of a healthy marriage relationship is to take it for granted and move it to the back burner. Barb and I know this from experience. When life speeds up and we are stretched in a dozen directions at once, the people closest to us are often the ones who are overlooked or shoved to the side.

One evening many years ago, when our two daughters were little girls, I arrived home from work in a semi-comatose state. Missy, our younger daughter, greeted me excitedly, "Daddy! Daddy! Daddy!" I didn't even notice her. She kept at it, saying "Daddy" about a dozen times. But I just kept walking.

Barb turned to Missy and said, "Honey, your daddy isn't home yet."

"Yes, he is," Missy argued innocently. "He's right there."

"You know that, Sarah knows that, even Katie the dog knows that. But your daddy doesn't know it yet."

That was just one of many times my out-of-whack priorities were harmful to my wife and daughters.

If we don't keep a tight rein on our priorities, we may find ourselves in the same frame of mind as a top national executive who said, "Reaching the level of business success that I have requires total commitment. If your family is too demanding, get a new family. That's what I did."[1] This guy didn't put his relationships on the back burner; he tossed them into the trash! It takes work and effort to keep our family relationships a top priority. It also takes sacrifice.

In their book *Fit to Be Tied*, Bill and Lynne Hybels wrote about the dangers of "crisis-mode living" in a marriage relationship. They defined crisis-mode living as "spending every moment of every day trying to figure out how to keep all your balls in the air and all your plates spinning. In crisis mode you keep running faster and faster, from project to project, deadline to deadline, quota to quota, meeting to meeting, sermon to sermon. Your RPMs keep creeping higher and higher until you hit the red line."[2]

What's the fallout from crisis-mode living? Your marriage relationship suffers. Energy needed for nurturing intimacy and resolving conflict instead goes into keeping our lives at a hectic pace. The Hybels continue:

> The problem arises when you spend too much time in crisis mode. That's when crisis mode goes from being a season of life to becoming a way of life. . . . In every other area of life, you become a miser; you hoard your energy, you

engage minimally, you touch superficially, you slide along the surface, you skim.

First you skim relationally. Your bond with your spouse that used to be strong and intimate becomes increasingly weak and distant. You hope he or she doesn't have a serious need because you don't have energy to deal with it. You hydro-plane over conflicts. You put Band-Aids on serious problems. You resort to quick fixes, and pretend things really aren't so bad.[3]

You may be asking, "If I'm supposed to give my marriage priority over my hurried schedule, how can I pull it off in a practical way? How can I find a balance between succeeding in my activities outside the home and still succeeding at home?"

I love the answer I received a number of years ago from a banker in South Dakota. At the time I talked to him about balancing work and family, he was in the middle of a pressure-packed farm crisis. His bank was foreclosing on farmers across the country, and bankers like him were perceived as the bad guys. It was not the kind of job you can simply walk away from at 5:00 P.M. every day. Here's what this man told me.

"Gary, I live twenty miles from my bank. I've determined the halfway point between work and home and have selected a specific telephone pole as a marker. When I leave the bank at night, I give myself the first ten miles, ending at that pole, to think about my bank, my customers, and my job. But when I pass that pole, I consciously switch my thinking to my family. I mentally prepare to greet them and spend time with them during my evening at home. And when I leave for work in the morning, I spend the first ten miles reflecting on my family. When I pass my marker, I begin to mentally prepare for the day at the bank."

It is not easy to master this mental and emotional discipline. But the rewards are great. If you want to relate well with your spouse, especially when you must work through a conflict, you need to make your relationship a priority over the baggage of busyness.

STEP 4: ASK OTHERS TO HOLD YOU ACCOUNTABLE

It takes effort and discipline to keep your heart prepared for dealing with conflicts in your marriage. Barb and I have discovered the great benefit of enlisting others to help us keep our marriage positive and growing. That's why we encourage you to draw close to a small group of Christian friends who will help you grow as a husband or wife by holding you accountable.

Way back in 1978, I realized my need for close companionship with a few men. I needed a place to just be myself as a man, a husband, and a father—not as a professional counselor. I wanted a few men to know me well enough to ask me the tough questions and help me keep Barb and our girls as top priority. So I began meeting every Tuesday at noon in the corner booth of an Italian restaurant with three close friends: Tim, Jerry, and Mike. We have been meeting together ever since.

During our weekly meetings, we have done everything from Bible studies to book discussions, from praying together to telling jokes. Confidentiality and mutual respect are a huge issue for us. What is said at that table stays at that table—period. We can be ourselves with each other, happy or hurting. We share our dreams with each other and hold each other accountable. To the outside world we are a physician, a financial advisor, a businessman, and a counselor. But when we meet, we leave our credentials at the door. We are just four guys who care about, listen to, and pray for each other.

In the fall of 1989, after having clocked about 12,000 hours in my career as a marriage and family therapist, I realized something about the men I was counseling. Most of them had the same needs my group of friends and I had. They needed supportive relationships with other men to help them stay on track as loving husbands, nurturing fathers, and growing Christians. Some men kept making counseling appointments with me not because they needed counseling, but because we had built a good relationship and they didn't want to see it end. They were desperate for a relationship that would help them and hold them accountable for being the men they really wanted to be.

In order to help some of the men I was counseling, I asked my three friends if I could invite about ten other guys to a weekly study. We tried it for a few months, and it took off. Since 1989, I have met every Wednesday morning with a group of men called CrossTrainers. About four years into our gatherings we added a noon group. Today, there are 500 to 600 men attending these two weekly groups, representing more than 140 churches. These are guys from every walk of life within a seventy-five-mile radius of Des Moines. One of two other teachers or I begin each meeting by summarizing a chapter in a contemporary Christian book. We then encourage men to get into small accountability groups with guys from their church or guys they meet at CrossTrainers. We talk about what we are learning, ask each other tough questions about our growth, and hold each other accountable.

Our goal in this ministry is not only to "train for the cross" or grow spiritually but also to "cross train" for our different roles as Christian husbands, dads, friends, and members of the community. One of the reasons CrossTrainers works is that we stress the importance of confidentiality, especially when a new man joins the group. God is using the group to change lives.

Surrounding yourself with an accountability group can help you become a hero in your home and beyond. Since the tragic events of September 11, 2001, we have all become acquainted with some of the heroes who gave their lives during the terrorist

attack on America. One of those heroes was Todd Beamer, a passenger aboard United Airlines Flight 93, which crashed in southern Pennsylvania. Beamer was among a group of passengers who
apparently challenged the terrorists aboard the flight and di-
verted the plane from its mission of destruction.

Todd Beamer was a committed Christian, a loving husband,
and a devoted father of two sons. (The couple's third child, a
daughter, was born four months after Todd's death.) Todd and
Lisa Beamer sought friendship and accountability as a couple and
as individuals. Barb and I had the privilege of meeting Lisa
Beamer during the summer of 2002. In her book, *Let's Roll!*, Lisa
tells about how she and Todd got involved in a church in New Jer-
sey just after they got married:

> One group that Todd and I became a part of was a Care
> Circle, several young couples who usually met once a
> week on Sunday evening to talk about life issues in relation
> to our faith. Sometimes our discussion centered around a
> book we had all agreed to read; often the conversation fo-
> cused on husband-and-wife relationships or other topics
> related to spiritual growth. The group was more than
> merely a gab session. We frequently prayed with and for
> each other, as various members experienced tremendous
> victories and horrible defeats, great achievements and
> traumatic events in their lives.[4]

Todd Beamer, a hard-working software salesman, also sought
the friendship, fellowship, and support of a small group of guys.
He wanted to make sure his heart was right and his priorities
were straight. Lisa Beamer continues:

> After we'd lived in New Jersey for a few years, most of our
> closest friendships revolved around our church and our

care group. Todd and several of the guys . . . started meeting for breakfast at 6:30 A.M. on Friday mornings in an accountability group. The group's primary purpose was to help the guys maintain a healthy balance between spiritual priorities and home/career responsibilities. They did everything together: played on the church softball team, did home improvement projects, and at least once a year went on a special guys-only weekend golf trip.

We had no idea how special those relationships would become to all of us.[5]

I am accountable to Barb, and she is accountable to me. But that isn't enough. We each rely on the closeness, support, and encouragement of trusted Christian friends to keep us moving ahead in our marriage. One of the wisest moves I ever made was asking six men to hold me accountable. The three men I have lunch with on Tuesdays hold me accountable. My sons-in-law, Scott and Cooper, hold me accountable. And author and speaker Steve Farrar holds me accountable. If something bad is brewing in my life, I may get it past one or two of those guys, but chances are I won't slip it past all six. Each of these men has *carte blanche* to ask me whatever they need to ask me. They don't control my life, but they help me guard my heart.

We all need people who will ask us the tough questions. Without that accountability, we can become isolated, and the chance for sin gaining a foothold in our lives and in our marriages increases dramatically.

In the course of preparing your heart for conflict resolution with your spouse, you may uncover some anger bubbling beneath the surface. Wherever there is hurt, there is some measure of anger. If it is not diffused, your anger will impede the process of healing. In the next chapter, Barb and I will coach you on how to deal with your anger.

9

Diffuse Your Anger

Brad was watching his college team's football game on TV Saturday afternoon, as he usually did. Every time Meg passed through the family room, she nagged her husband about getting the yard work done, as she usually did. When the rival team scored the winning touchdown against his team, Brad did something he had never done before: He threw his empty iced-tea glass at the television set. Luckily, the glass was plastic. But it ricocheted off the TV and knocked a picture frame to the hardwood floor, shattering the glass. When Meg hurried in to see what happened, Brad glared at her. "Don't even ask," he snarled. Then he stalked into the garage, leaving Meg with her mouth hanging open.

─────────── ❦ ───────────

Ellie was behind schedule for getting herself and her two preschoolers out the door to ladies' Bible study. She was a small group leader at the study, and she didn't want to be late. Then Ellie's two-year-old daughter filled her diaper at the last minute, requiring a complete outfit change. As Ellie was doing that, her four-year-old boy got into the refrigerator and spilled half a pitcher of Kool-Aid on the kitchen floor. When she discovered the mess, Ellie yelled at her son angrily. "You're just like your dad, always getting into stuff you can't handle." Then she burst into tears. She wished she could take the words back as soon as she said them.

Joel arrived home to his wife and three kids after a very stressful day. Walking into the house, everything just hit him wrong. The kitchen hadn't been cleaned up from lunch, and LuAnn hadn't started dinner preparation yet. Toys were strewn everywhere. LuAnn greeted him warmly, but all Joel could do was mutter, "Well, you've had a productive day." Then he retreated to the bedroom to change clothes.

Offenses in a marriage relationship produce hurts, and hurts often bubble over into anger. We talked about the chain reaction of hurt and anger in chapter 3. Sometimes our anger simmers beneath the surface; sometimes it explodes. Sometimes it is directed at our spouse, sometimes we take it out on someone or something else. If you are going to successfully work through your conflicts and find healing as a couple, you must learn to diffuse your anger. (See the diagram in figure 9.) In this chapter, Barb and I will help you with this stage in the process of exercising forgiving love.

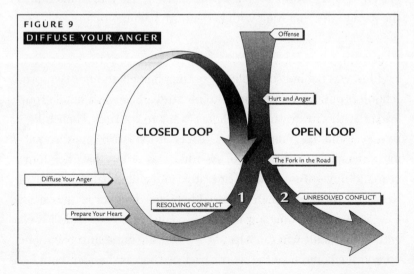

FIGURE 9
DIFFUSE YOUR ANGER

Offense

Hurt and Anger

CLOSED LOOP

OPEN LOOP

The Fork in the Road

Diffuse Your Anger

RESOLVING CONFLICT 1

2 UNRESOLVED CONFLICT

Prepare Your Heart

The apostle Paul made it clear that the emotion of anger is not intrinsically bad. He wrote, "'Don't sin by letting anger gain control over you.' Don't let the sun go down while you are still angry, for anger gives a mighty foothold to the Devil" (Ephesians 4:26-27). Notice that Paul didn't say, "Don't be angry." Rather, he warned that anger has the potential to lead us into sin if we respond to it by offending others.

So how can we be angry but not sin when someone has hurt us? The answer is found in learning the distinction between anger and aggression. Anger is an emotion, a feeling. Aggression is a potentially harmful behavior, an act of the will. Anger can be expressed in a God-honoring way. Jesus, for example, displayed righteous anger when he threw the moneychangers out of God's temple in Jerusalem. Anger can also stimulate us to resolve a conflict that has been brewing for some time.

How do we diffuse our anger before it grows into aggression? Here are several biblical guidelines.

DEAL WITH ANGER IN A TIMELY WAY

Don't let the sun go down while you are still angry. In other words, don't ignore it. Make plans and take steps to diffuse your anger in a timely manner, before it mushrooms into resentment, bitterness, or depression.

People make two common mistakes in dealing with anger. First, they allow it to boil over instead of halting the conversation or argument and taking time to calm down. When you feel the heat of anger rising in you or when you see signs of anger in your spouse, that should be a warning sign: *Anger building! Time-out!* If anger sparks in you quickly, you need to slow down and confront your anger in an appropriate way.

The second mistake is waiting too long to deal with anger. Many people count to ten, let off a little steam, and then don't feel angry anymore. So they assume there is nothing to deal with. That's a myth. Chances are, the anger is still simmering inside them, waiting for another opportunity to boil over. As soon as the anger factor knifes into your marriage, deal with it. If you put it off, it only becomes more difficult to resolve.

Don't be too literal about dealing with your anger before bedtime. Barb and I heard about a couple who stayed up for two and a half days working through a conflict because the Bible said they shouldn't go to sleep angry! Trying to resolve conflicts late at night is almost always a mistake. As the evening wears on, most of us get fatigued. Sometimes getting proper rest will help you settle things better in the morning.

COOL DOWN BEFORE SPEAKING UP

"Here we go again. We always do it your way. I'm sick of it—and sick of you!"

"I can't believe you did that again! *Grrr!* You really tick me off!"

"I give up. You'll never change. I have to do everything around here."

Behind each of those verbal fireballs is a frustrated, angry spouse. Most times, such explosions are counterproductive to resolving marital conflict. Dealing with anger in a timely manner doesn't mean just "going off" by venting your feelings indiscriminately. Cutting, anger-driven words only produce more hurt. Instead, take time to "cool your jets," as we used to say. Work through the issue with patience and discernment.

We get impatient when we react in anger without thinking. An emotional *reaction* comes from the gut; it's automatic and sometimes involuntary. A *response* is conscious, planned, and purposeful. It takes longer to come up with a response, but it's much more effective than a brusque reaction. As some wise person once said, the difference between a reaction and a response is about three seconds.

Furthermore, pausing to cool down will help you determine if you may have contributed as much or more to the problem as your spouse did. Take time to humble yourself and exercise discernment. Take a close look inside yourself to see if you have offended your spouse. I believe this is what Jesus meant when he said, "Hypocrite! First get rid of the log from your own eye; then perhaps you will see well enough to deal with the speck in your friend's eye" (Matthew 7:5).

CONTROL YOUR TONGUE

Staring at her husband, Angie's eyes seemed to glaze over. After Jason's twenty-minute verbal tirade, all Angie could say was, "I can't hear you."

I can certainly hear him, I thought, watching the exchange. *So can the people in my waiting room and in the next office.* Jason's anger had just erupted all over his wife. At one time, these two people were happy and optimistic, planning a great life together. Now there was pain in their eyes, despair in their hearts, and futility in their communication.

Jason's explosion led me to offer a rather unusual intervention. "I want to describe what I just saw," I told the couple. "Now, this may sound a little gross, Jason, but your outburst was kind of like vomiting all over Angie."

"That's *really* gross, Doc," Jason snapped angrily.

"I know," I said. "That's exactly my point. As gross as that word picture is, that's how gross your communication sounded."

"That's why I couldn't hear you, Jason," Angie interjected, tears rolling down her cheeks. "When you explode like that, I can't get past my own hurt to hear what you're saying. I hear you screaming and see the hate in your eyes, and I shut down."

Angie and Jason were the epitome of a couple frustrated by their inability to manage their God-given emotions. Instead of controlling their anger, they just let it fly. Angie went on to tell me that whenever Jason flew into a rage, she flashed back to her angry father and shut down, just as she did as a child.

Like Jason, many of us have the problem of not controlling our tongue. That little muscle inside your mouth is capable of doing great good and great harm. You have the power to heal a broken relationship with your spouse or burn it to the ground with what you say and how you say it. Proverbs 18:21 says, "The tongue can kill or nourish life." The apostle James wrote, "The tongue is a small thing, but what enormous damage it can do. A tiny spark can set a great forest on fire" (James 3:5).

How can you control your tongue? Here are several suggestions.

Slow down your communication. Sometimes we get so charged up with anger that the mouth runs off before the brain is in gear. Consciously and purposely speak at a slower pace when you are angry, giving yourself time to think before you speak.

Give your spouse permission to help you keep angry words in check. When you are not in the heat of an angry conflict, ask your spouse to alert you when your words are getting out of control. Agree on some kind of signal (such as having your spouse raise a finger to his or her mouth) that will remind you to keep your tongue under control.

After a confrontation, ask your spouse if your words offended him or her. Listen and learn, then put your spouse's input into practice to help you develop healthier conflict-resolution skills.

Practice gentle words. Proverbs 15:1 promises, "A gentle answer turns away wrath, but harsh words stir up anger." Gentleness and patience, especially during a conflict, can soften the delivery of your message so your spouse will hear you and respond positively.

A significant aspect to diffusing anger is how you talk to yourself about the conflicts and hurts in your relationship. Barb will explain how this works and provide some helpful tips.

WATCH YOUR SELF-TALK

Have you ever caught yourself talking to yourself? We all do it, of course. At times you will mutter something to yourself aloud. If someone hears you, you may sheepishly explain, "Oh, I was just thinking out loud." But most of the time, self-talk is internal. It is the conscious thought process continually going on inside our heads.

Those who study language tell us that most people speak at the rate of 150 to 200 words per minute. In contrast, research indicates that self-talk can run at the rate of about 1,300 words per minute. On the basis of sheer volume alone, your self-talk has a powerful impact on your emotional and behavioral responses. So when it comes to marital conflict, hurt, and anger, you need to make sure your self-talk is positive and factual.

Any episode of self-talk begins with what we call a triggering event. It may be something a person says, an object we see, a scene we witness, a fragrance, a sound, or any number of other stimuli. When the trigger occurs, our minds start racing at 1,300 words per minute trying to interpret what we have received. In other words, we begin a high-speed, internal monologue trying to make sense of the triggering event.

For example, in one of the examples earlier in the chapter, LuAnn's husband, Joel, walks into the house after work. Seeing the kids' toys scattered throughout the house and lunch dishes still piled in the kitchen sink, Joel just shakes his head and mutters to his wife, "Well, you've had a productive day." Then he leaves LuAnn standing in the kitchen as he goes to change out of his work clothes.

Immediately LuAnn self-talks her way through the episode: *Joel doesn't value all that I do for him and the kids. He has no idea how hard I work all day long. He thinks I should have been more productive today. He sees only what didn't get done; he doesn't notice what I have done. He thinks I should be able to keep the house spotless even though I'm outnumbered three to one by kids who work hard to mess it up.*

This automatic thought process trips an emotional response based on how we interpret the event. It's a chain reaction, and it can all happen in a handful of heartbeats. LuAnn's self-talk has left her angry with Joel for his insensitivity to her daily tasks and his lack of appreciation for how hard she tries.

However, an emotional response, such as anger, isn't the end of the chain reaction. Your emotions will always give rise to some kind of behavioral response. You may cry, laugh, fight back, kick the dog, withdraw, overeat, drink too much, or whatever. Some people pull the covers over their heads and sleep for hours on end. Others fidget, pace, or drum their fingers.

LuAnn's behavioral response is to "go on strike" for a few minutes. Instead of scurrying around picking up toys or starting to prepare dinner to please Joel, she goes into the family room and sits down with the kids, who are watching a video.

Our behavior results from an emotional response based on self-talk triggered by a specific event—or combination of events. Here's what the chain reaction looks like:

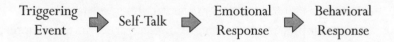

Triggering Event ➡ Self-Talk ➡ Emotional Response ➡ Behavioral Response

But here's the problem. Some of our emotional and behavioral responses are irrational because sometimes our self-talk— our perception of the triggering event—is inaccurate. For example, LuAnn misinterpreted Joel's actions and comment about the house when he walked in. He wasn't criticizing her; he was trying to acknowledge from the mess that his wife had had a hard day. But for LuAnn, something important got lost in the self-talk. Bottom line: At times your angry feelings and behavior may be a legitimate response to an event, but at other times they may be the inappropriate result of faulty self-talk.

One of the major ways to diffuse anger in your conflicts, therefore, is to control your self-talk. Here are four helpful steps to help you do that.

1. Acknowledge that self-talk happens in you. Everybody uses self-talk. You may not be aware that you are doing it, but you are.

2. Recognize when self-talk is happening. Look at the diagram again—the self-talk happens between the event and your response to it.

3. Challenge your self-talk to see if it is rational (supported by evidence) or irrational (not supported by evidence). Here are some questions to ask yourself:

* What evidence exists to support my anger in this situation?
* What past events might be contributing to how I'm feeling?
* What might be my spouse's viewpoint on this issue?
* Do my spouse's past actions match how I interpreted his or her recent behavior, or do they suggest something different?
* What are some alternative interpretations to this situation?
* Have I unfairly judged my spouse by assuming I know what he or she is thinking?

After careful evaluation, you may realize that your interpretation of the situation really is the correct one and your feelings of anger are justified. But sometimes you will discover that your anger is irrational because you have been operating from false assumptions about the triggering event. As LuAnn thought about Joel's comment, she wondered if she had misread his response. He had never criticized her before when the house was in disarray. Joel confirmed her evaluation when he walked into the family room after changing clothes and said, "Looks like everybody had a hard day today, including me. So I'm treating everyone to pizza. Who's ready to go?"

4. Replace inaccurate self-talk with accurate self-talk. Whenever you discover that your anger is the result of a misperception of the triggering event, backtrack and talk yourself through the correct view of what happened. You'll be surprised at how your anger evaporates. Even before LuAnn and Joel left for the restaurant, she had adjusted her self-talk: *Joel was sounding a little down when he got home because he had a rough day at work. He wasn't displeased with me; he was empathizing with me over my hard day.* LuAnn, Joel, and the kids had a great evening together.

I love what the apostle Paul says in Romans 12:2, "Don't copy the behavior and customs of this world, but let God transform you into a new person by changing the way you think." Don't give in to the automatic self-talk that races through your head. Challenge your thoughts. Take every thought captive and make it obedient to Christ (see 2 Corinthians 10:5).

Our self-talk is part of who we are. We need to understand those messages and challenge them so we control our anger instead of being controlled by it.

GIVE UP YOUR RIGHT TO REVENGE

Like LuAnn and Joel, sometimes your marital conflicts are a case of mistaken perception and faulty self-talk. But often your anger is valid because there really was an offense—and it hurt. When this happens, another important element of controlling your anger is to let go of any sense of exacting revenge. The apostle Peter admonished believers, "Don't repay evil for evil. Don't retaliate when people say unkind things about you. Instead, pay them back with a blessing. That is what God wants you to do, and he will bless you for it" (1 Peter 3:9).

Let's say, for the sake of illustration, that Joel really was critical of LuAnn when he came home that day. Imagine LuAnn following him into the bedroom for this heated exchange.

"You looked and sounded displeased when you walked in, Joel. What was that all about?"

"I looked and sounded displeased, LuAnn, because I *am* displeased. The house is a mess. Why can't you have things straight when I get home? What's so hard about picking up a few toys and keeping the kitchen tidy?"

"You just try it for a week, Joel, and you'll find out what's so hard about it." Then she stormed out of the room.

When your spouse's offense hurts and angers you, the natural tendency is to look for a way to get even. You may be tempted to hurl an insult, or you may plot a more intricate revenge. LuAnn may be considering several options for "payback." She could prepare a slapdash dinner, something Joel doesn't really like. She could make it quite clear at bedtime that there will be no romance tonight or anytime soon. She could purposely lighten up on the housework for the next few days just to show Joel how untidy it can get.

The problem is that repaying one offense with another offense only fans the flame of conflict and makes it worse. At some point, one of you has to stop the cycle and, as the apostle Peter wrote, give a blessing instead. When you do that, you are clearing the way for diffusing the anger and healing the hurt.

Here are two other ways LuAnn and Joel could have handled their conflict. First, let's consider how Joel could have diffused LuAnn's anger during their bedroom discussion.

"You looked and sounded displeased when you walked in, Joel. What was that all about?"

Joel looked away for a moment. Then he said, "I guess I reacted poorly to the condition of the house. I know you work hard to keep things tidy around here. Maybe we should talk about how I can be of more help."

"I would appreciate that, Joel. If you could spend some time with the kids right now, I'll put something together for dinner. After the kids are in bed, perhaps we can talk about this."

Second, following the confrontation in the bedroom, LuAnn, instead of plotting her revenge, could have diffused her anger in several ways. She could have put together a dinner Joel likes to convey "no hard feelings." After the kids were down for the night, she might suggest—in a pleasant tone—that she and Joel talk about his earlier critical comment.

You won't be able to talk about a conflict if one or both of you is still steaming with anger. But once you diffuse your anger, the next stage of conflict resolution is to communicate clearly about the offense, your hurt, and your feelings. In the next chapter we will provide some helpful direction.

10

Communicate Your Concerns

A good deal of the marital communication Barb and I hear about is like elevator talk. You know how it is when you step into an elevator with a bunch of strangers. You avoid eye contact, either gazing down at your shoes or watching the floor numbers change above the door. Conversation, what little there may be, is usually no deeper than exchanging opinions about the weather. And as soon as you reach your floor, it's over with, and you're out of there.

Sadly, many married couples don't get much deeper in their communication than elevator talk. Communication is typically the first issue to come up during marriage counseling. In survey after survey, couples rate difficulties in communication as a major problem in their relationship. I remember one wife who said, "He tuned me out years ago. He just doesn't listen to me or hear me. He's so preoccupied with work, TV, sports, and his stock portfolio." Her husband retorted, "Well, I tell you when I'll be late for dinner, don't I?"

Here were two people living in the same house, but the husband might as well have been deaf for all he was hearing and understanding from his wife. It had been years since they had talked about the important things in their lives, things necessary to knit a close relationship. And we hear the same kind of complaint from husbands whose wives are so absorbed in their children, their social circle, church activities, and/or work that little time remains for sharing deeply with their husbands.

Communicating your concerns is absolutely necessary to the process of healing the relationship. (See diagram in figure 10.) In fact, communication is absolutely vital to the health of your relationship even when there isn't a conflict. And if you struggle at communicating in times of peace, it will be even more difficult in times of conflict. So Barb and I want to coach you in seven basic communication principles that will not only help you resolve conflicts but also equip you for enriching the intimacy of your marriage relationship day to day.

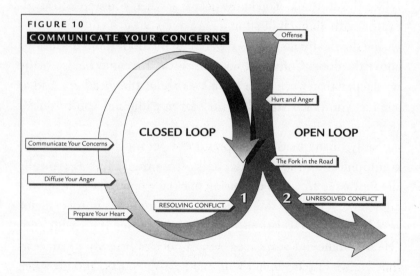

FIGURE 10

COMMUNICATE YOUR CONCERNS

Offense

Hurt and Anger

CLOSED LOOP   OPEN LOOP

Communicate Your Concerns

The Fork in the Road

Diffuse Your Anger

RESOLVING CONFLICT   1   2   UNRESOLVED CONFLICT

Prepare Your Heart

PRINCIPLE 1:
CHECK YOUR RELATIONAL TEMPERATURE

When you go into the doctor's office for your annual checkup or for a physical problem, the nurse always checks your vital signs—blood pressure, temperature, pulse rate. If anything is wrong internally, such as an infection, there's a good chance the doctor will find a clue in these basic measurements. Similarly, for a number of years Barb and I have checked the vital signs in our marriage to both diagnose and prevent conflicts. It's one of the best ways we know to open up communication that will lead to healing.

Here's what we do. Every four to six weeks, we pose two questions to each other. We call it *taking our relational temperature.* We're not legalistic about doing it, and it's not something we feel we have to schedule on the calendar. Often we will have this discussion during a walk together or at the end of a date night. Sometimes these questions will come up when one or both of us feel some tension in the relationship. Whenever we make a point to ask and respond to these two questions, we are able to cut conflicts off at the pass. We encourage you to use these questions periodically to check your vital signs as a couple.

1. How am I doing as a spouse? When I ask Barb how I'm doing as a husband, I'm not fishing for compliments, although she is generous to provide them. I'm looking for honest feedback. I want to know where I am missing the mark as her husband or offending her in some way. I give Barb *carte blanche* to tell it as it is, and she expects the same from me when she asks, "How am I doing as a wife?" We usually go away from these discussions knowing exactly what we can do to prevent or disarm conflicts in our marriage.

This question allows the person closest to you, your lifetime partner, to lovingly point out any blind spots. Perhaps you have shifted from focusing on the Lord and your spouse due to other demands in your daily schedule: work, church activities, hobbies, etc. If anything is taking you captive, if the good things you are involved in outside the relationship are hindering the best things in your relationship, it should come to light when you ask each other this first question.

2. What do you need from me? This is not only a question about things like helping with household chores or finding a lost article in the house. Typical of the answers we hear from one another are things such as "more time with you"; "a little more patience"; "affection—a wink, a smile, a hug"; or "during this pressure-packed week, I need you to pray with me." Being proactive about uncovering your spouse's needs will help you preempt many conflicts. It is also a straightforward way to communicate that you care about meeting needs in your relationship.

Taking your relational temperature is the foundational component to communication in your marriage. It's more than talking and listening; it's sharing your thoughts, feelings, and needs. Yes, it can be risky. You may get an answer you don't want to hear, one that will require a change on your part. But without this kind of vulnerability and risk there is little opportunity for growth.

PRINCIPLE 2:
ADJUST TO YOUR SPOUSE'S GENDER STYLE

When Bill and Eileen came to see me, they said they had hit an impasse in their relationship. After eleven years of marriage, Eileen felt isolated and alone. Bill had courted her well enough in the early days of their marriage, and Eileen had been loving and attentive to Bill's needs. But over the last several years, their relationship had lost much of its excitement. The marriage was on autopilot, and this couple was just coasting along. They were both busy in their careers and found most of their companionship in friends and coworkers. Eileen was ready to trade Bill in for a new model because of his consistent unwillingness to talk to her and listen to her.

As we began to unravel the causes of their conflict in counseling sessions, it became obvious to me that they had a fundamental problem: Eileen treated Bill as if he were woman, and Bill expected Eileen to relate to him as if she were a man. Each expected the other to communicate in his or her own gender style, and since that was impossible, they were frustrated and growing more distant in their marriage.

Men and women communicate differently. That's just how God wired us. In their classic book *Love Is a Decision*, Gary Smalley and John Trent refer to studies indicating that "the average woman speaks roughly 25,000 words a day, while the average man speaks only 12,500."[1]

The implication for Bill and Eileen was clear. Bill was using up about 12,000 words of his daily allotment with his coworkers and clients at the office. When he came home, he didn't have a lot of communication left in him. But Eileen, who also used about 12,000 words at work each day, was just hitting her stride by the time she arrived home. Bill was verbally worn-out and treated Eileen as if she didn't want to talk much either. At the same time, Eileen was ready to chat the evening away and imposed her gender style on Bill. Is it any wonder they had unresolved conflicts?

How can a husband and wife adjust to each other's gender style of communication? It helps a great deal just to be aware that a difference exists. As you sharpen your awareness of this difference, continually ask yourself, "What can I do to meet my spouse's communication need?" (For more help, see *The Five Love Needs of Men and Women,* a book about how to identify and meet the top five love needs of husbands and wives.)

Wives, realize that your husband is probably not as adept at or perhaps not as deeply interested in frequent and extended conversation as you are. It is okay to be home together or driving somewhere together and not be constantly talking about something. And it will allow your husband to focus his communication on those times when you need to talk through some issues or conflicts.

Husbands, get a clue that your wife needs to talk about things more than you do. You may need to save some of your "word power" during the day to spend on your wife. As you make her communication needs a priority, you may even find that you have a greater capacity for talking than you realize.

There are exceptions to the rule, of course. Some men are more skilled and interested in conversation than their wives. But it is remarkable how often we hear about women who want more communication and men who want less. Nearly daily on our national radio program, *America's Family Coaches . . . LIVE!,* women will call with the desire to connect daily with their husband in communication. The key is to be sensitive to your spouse's communication style.

PRINCIPLE 3:
CHOOSE THE RIGHT TIME AND PLACE

Your wife is frantically preparing an elegant party for guests who will arrive in less than an hour. The kids and the dog are running in and out of the house. The television is blaring from the family room. If you think this is the time to pull up a stool in the kitchen and say something like, "Honey, we need to have a serious talk," think again.

Your husband has just finished his third day of overtime in a row and he's dead on his feet. He snoozes through the late news in the recliner and can barely drag himself to the bedroom. As you climb into bed together, you may be tempted to say, "Dear, we haven't talked much lately. Can we chat a little about what's going on in our lives?" Warning: Don't yield to that temptation.

When it comes to successful communication in general or talking through a conflict in particular, timing and setting are vitally important. A friend once named two major components of healthy marital communication: skill and time. You need to exercise effective sharing, listening, and connecting skills in marriage communication, and you need to make it a priority in your schedule. You must be willing to initiate time with your spouse and be quick to respond when he or she takes the initiative. And when the timing doesn't work for you, be sure to suggest a time that does work.

Communication is a process that allows a couple to express their hearts to each other. It involves both expressing themselves to one another and attentively listening to one another. In order for this to happen effectively, you need time that isn't crowded with other activities and responsibilities, and you need a place that is free from distraction and interruption. When loving communication happens in a quiet, unhurried atmosphere, a husband and wife establish a sense of emotional intimacy that allows the relationship to blossom.

My parents modeled this principle for me beautifully. Every weekday evening, my dad arrived home from work around 5:30. We four kids would run to greet him, and then we would return to watching TV, riding bikes, or doing homework. Meanwhile, my mom and dad would sit in our family room for about an hour and talk. The kids weren't invited, but sometimes I would go into the kitchen and peek in on them unseen. I remember my dad and mom talking about some pretty serious family business and problems they were experiencing. But I also remember seeing them laugh together and just enjoy each other's company. It went on for an hour every day before dinner.

Barb and I have followed that model in our own home so that Sarah and Missy would grow up learning marital communication from our example. We needed that time together, but as the girls got older, the interruptions became more frequent. We finally established a rule: no interrupting your parents during this time unless you're bleeding, broken, or bruised. It worked. We rarely were interrupted from then on.

Whether you are in the midst of resolving a conflict or just getting through day-to-day living, you are wise to develop a pattern of unhurried, daily interaction with each other. Find a time that is convenient to both of you—schedule it in your calendar if you have to. Designate a special place that is free of interruption. Such a commitment will not only help to avert some conflicts, it will also establish a pattern for ongoing times of significant communication.

PRINCIPLE 4:
SHARE THOUGHTS, FEELINGS, AND NEEDS

Once you find the appropriate time and place to communicate, what do you say to each other? We believe there are three important components to any message you share with your spouse: thoughts, feelings, and needs. It is the combination of these ingredients that makes for meaningful sharing in times of peace or conflict.

Men and women are most likely to feel connected when they share thoughts, feelings, and needs with each other. The key is knowing in which order to share these components. Barb and I have discovered that men and women are wired differently in this area also. So we will coach you separately on how to communicate with your spouse in a way that harmonizes with his or her communication style. I will share with the women first, then Barb will talk to the men.

Communicating with Your Husband
When you want to communicate effectively with your husband, the best order is information, feelings, then needs. When you follow this order, you are cooperating with the way God has wired your husband.

Share what you think about the issue. Wives, your husband needs information—content, a bottom line—and he usually needs that first. It is important for you to share what is on your mind about the topic or conflict in question. This will include both objective and subjective information plus your own insights, perceptions, ideas, values, and biases. The information element of communication may sound like this:

* "Your mom and dad are expecting us to fly out for the holidays. But if we do, I will miss Christmas with my parents for the third year in a row. I don't want to miss this opportunity to be with them. Dad hasn't been doing well lately and . . . well, you know . . . he won't be with us many more years."

* "I have a different perspective about our financial situation, so I disagree with the decision you want to make about our investments."

* "In my judgment, a midnight curfew for the weekends is too lenient. The kids can still have a good time with their friends and be home by 10:00 P.M."

Share how you feel about the issue. Once you have shared the bottom line with your husband, you can move on to sharing your feelings. Everything we think about is attached to one or more emotions: fear, pride, joy, sadness, frustration, betrayal, rejection, anger, anxiety, anticipation, contentment, depression, and so on. Here's how your feelings might be added to the "thought statements" above:

* "I really love seeing my parents, especially at the holidays. I would feel a lot of remorse if we didn't make the trip this year."

* "I'm frustrated that you called our financial advisor without talking to me about your concerns. It makes me feel as if I am out of the loop and uninformed."

* "When the kids are out so late on the weekend, I am very afraid of what they might get into. I want to protect them

from stepping beyond their capacity to make good decisions at this age."

Share what you need from your spouse. As you express your thoughts and reveal your emotions in communication, also state what you need from your husband in the situation. You are a partnership. You have committed before God to share each other's burdens. But it is difficult for your husband to help carry the load if you don't tell him what you need. Notice how the following statements add the expression of needs to the thought and feeling statements above.

* "Will you please talk to your parents and see if we can come out after Christmas so I won't miss seeing my parents?"
* "I know you are anxious about our financial plan. I want to honor that, but please promise me that you won't make a major financial decision without consulting me. And I need you to listen to me when we talk about our money."
* "I want us to decide on a reasonable curfew and then sit down with the kids together and explain our reasoning behind it."

Now Barb will share from her perspective and experience how a man can most effectively communicate with his wife.

Communicating with Your Wife

Men, your wife requires the same components of communication you do—thoughts, feelings, needs—but not in the same order. She needs to hear your feelings on the issue first, then your thoughts, and finally what you need to reach a solution. I guarantee that if you grasp what I am about to teach you for connecting with your wife, it will literally transform your marriage relationship! Here is my spin on how to communicate with your wife.

Connect with her heart. When you have a conflict with your wife, you may be tempted to move quickly from the offense to the solution. Gather the facts, assess the damage, fix the problem—most men are good at that. For example, Lacey tells Jon that she is hurt and angry because he signed her up for a committee at church without asking her first. Jon says, "No problem. I'll call the chairman and withdraw your name. And I'll never do that again." Problem solved, end of discussion. But that's not the end of the discussion or of the conflict. Jon has not addressed the hurt in Lacey's heart.

The first step in communicating positively with your wife is to connect with her emotions before dealing with the details of the offense. How do you do that? Assure her that you hear her pain. For example, Jon could have said something to Lacey like, "I see that I really hurt you by what I did. That was really insensitive of me. Tell me more about how you feel." If you don't hear your wife's heart first, she will feel misunderstood and frustrated. But when you ask her what she is feeling, she is more likely to feel heard. She will be able to process her frustration verbally, which will allow her to move to the next phase—thinking about the facts.

Connect with the facts. Once you understand the emotions your wife is experiencing, she will be able to look at the facts more clearly. The issue will move from her heart to her head. As she feels heard and is comforted by your concern over her hurt, she is better able to receive your thoughts and ideas. For example, after connecting with how Lacey feels, Jon might say, "When I heard about the committee position, I thought it was something you might enjoy. And I think your skills would be a plus to the committee. Is this something you might want to do in the future?"

Connect with a solution. After you have connected with your wife's emotions and discussed the facts, you may want to supply some ideas or options that will lead to a solution to the conflict. For example, Jon might say, "I was wrong to act without consulting you. If you like, I will call the chairman, apologize for speaking out of turn, and withdraw your name. Or if you have some interest in serving on the committee, I could get more information for you. What would you like me to do?" Such an approach lets your wife know that you want to help resolve the hurtful situation.

PRINCIPLE 5:
TUNE IN AND LISTEN TO YOUR SPOUSE

Have you heard the story about Walter and Harriet? Walter, well into his eighties, was an incessant talker. From sunup to sundown, he kept up a constant stream of chatter about nothing of importance. Harriet, his wife of sixty plus years, had long since stopped listening to him. She had learned the art of nodding and humming occasionally so Walter thought she was paying attention.

One day Harriet took Walter out for a drive. As usual, he droned on and on, barely taking a breath. When Harriet made a sharp left turn, the passenger door suddenly flew open and Walter tumbled out. Oblivious to what had just happened, Harriet drove on.

Fortunately, two police officers saw the whole thing. While one attended to poor Walter, the other raced after Harriet and pulled her over.

"Was I speeding, Officer?" she asked as the policeman approached.

"No, ma'am, you weren't speeding," he said. "But when you turned the corner a few blocks back, your husband fell out of the car."

"Thank goodness!" Harriet exclaimed. "I thought I had just gone deaf!"

We chuckle at this story, but on the serious side, Harriet and Walter represent a lot of married couples who just don't listen to each other. Some us have learned the fine art of "selective hearing," tuning each other out and only pretending to hear.

The Bible provides us with a simple guideline for all our relationships: "My dear brothers and sisters, be quick to listen, slow to speak, and slow to get angry. Your anger can never make things right in God's sight" (James 1:19-20). That says it well, doesn't it? Quick to listen, slow to speak, and slow to become angry.

If you are quick to listen, you will be more concerned about hearing and understanding your spouse than about getting your point across or winning the argument. Many times, the key to resolving a conflict is simply to listen to your spouse and seek to understand his or her position on the issue. When you both practice this discipline, you will probably be able to see things more clearly and reach a point of agreement.

Gary and I coach husbands and wives to listen *actively*. Active listening begins with eye contact. When your spouse is sharing with you, turn away from the newspaper, magazine, TV, or anything else and lock onto his or her eyes. When you avoid eye contact, you are conveying, "What you are about to say isn't as important as this important issue I am focusing on." Eye contact is vital to healthy marital communication. Eyes are the windows to the soul.

Body language is also important to active listening. When you face your spouse, lean toward him or her, and occasionally nod your affirmation, your body is saying, "I'm really interested in what you are saying. You have my full attention." This is a concrete way to honor your spouse.

Research has shown that body language and tone of voice make up over 90 percent of our communication. Our actual words make up the rest. What you say can be drowned out by how you say it. And how you listen can communicate volumes about your interest in your spouse's words.

PRINCIPLE 6:
SHARE WHAT YOUR SPOUSE NEEDS TO HEAR

Earlier in our marriage, Gary and I sometimes hit a wall in our communication and couldn't figure out why. We are both well educated, and we have always gotten along well. But sometimes we just couldn't understand each other, and this lack of understanding often erupted in conflicts.

After eight or nine years of marriage, we realized that we were not telling each other what we needed to hear. When I reported to Gary about my day or shared some information, I included all the details that I found important and interesting. For example, if I went to lunch with some girlfriends, I told Gary what happened minute by minute: who was there, what was said, what kind of day I had, what music was playing in the background, and on and on. In other words, I communicated to Gary what every woman loves to hear—the details—treating Gary as if he were one of my girlfriends.

In the meantime, Gary would be thinking, *Come on, Barb, get to the point.* As with most men, Gary isn't very interested in all the little details. Men by nature are more "bottom line" in their communication style. They need to hear the main point, see the big picture. Gary says that when he goes out to lunch with the guys, he barely remembers what he ate, let alone what someone else ate or wore. His report might sound like this: "We had a good lunch, shared some great stuff, and plan to meet again." End of story.

That was the other side of our communication problem. When Gary shared with me, I would be frustrated because he glossed over the details that are so important to me. Like most women, I like to hear all the interesting tidbits. But since Gary is a bottom-line communicator, that's usually what I got from him.

After years of frustration, it finally dawned on us that we had different styles of communicating because we needed different things from communication. While I was consumed with all the elements of the message, Gary was searching for the main point. And when he delivered his to-the-point message, I was left hungering for more heart.

A man's approach to communication is often called the pyramid style of sharing information. When journalists write news stories, they start at the top of the pyramid with the main point: "Tornado claims hundreds of lives"; "Pentagon steps up war effort"; "Famous actor dies." Subsequent paragraphs give additional information, from the most important to the most trivial. Many men are content just to read each headline and opening paragraph in the newspaper. And that's often how they communicate with their wives.

Invert the pyramid, and you see how many women share information—not like a journalist but like a novelist. We gradually unfold the plot, giving all kinds of details and sidelights, adding to the story layer by layer, and eventually working our way to the main point by the end of the story.

Communication between Gary and me has greatly improved over the years as we came to understand what each of us needs when we talk together. When we sit down to chat about our day, I give him several "bullets" of information, which satisfies his need to know up front what we're talking about. I will continue with the details to the extent that he is interested. But when Gary shares, he has learned to give me all sorts of information, weaving in as many secondary issues as he can remember before delivering the punch line. We both feel fulfilled with this type of communication.

When dealing with conflict, we use the same approach. I will say something like, "Gary, I need to talk to you about the way you spoke to me this morning." I get right to the point, no beating around the bush. He can handle it because he knows my agenda immediately. He typically responds, "Tell me what you're concerned about." With that we begin to discuss and resolve the issue.

But if Gary approaches me with the same directness, he knows he might wound me. So he is more apt to ease me into the topic by saying something like, "Barb, I need to talk with you about something that's been bothering me." This statement alerts me that he has something to say, but it meets my need to go through the process instead of jumping right to the bottom line.

Neither of these styles of communicating is right or wrong, and neither is exclusively male or female. We have known women who are "bottom liners" and men who enjoy the details. The point is to understand your spouse's needs in communication and give yourself to meeting that need. As with the other principles in this chapter, doing so will improve your communication, and better communication facilitates conflict resolution.

PRINCIPLE 7:
LISTEN FOR THE UNDERLYING ISSUE

"Ruth, I don't want to go to your mother's today for dinner. I have a lot of work to do around the yard."

If Ruth takes Brent's comment at face value, it sounds pretty good. It's true that Brent has yard work to do. It's also true that if he goes to his mother-in-law's, he won't get it done. But knowing Brent as she does, Ruth senses he is communicating something else nonverbally. The context of Brent's comment helps Ruth perceive the underlying issue in her husband's comment.

Whenever Ruth's family gets together for weekend dinners, the same things usually happen. Ruth's dad jumps all over her mom, and she complains that he is always glued to sports on TV. They both gripe about not seeing the grandkids often enough. When Brent and Ruth leave, they are both frustrated by the negative atmosphere. Ruth is caught in the middle, feeling defensive about her parents yet agreeing with Brent that their visits are generally unpleasant. She understands his reticence to "blow an afternoon" when it is the only time he has for yard work.

So is Brent's "excuse" about needing to do yard work valid? Technically, yes. But is it the whole story? No, and both Brent and Ruth know it. Brent is really trying to avoid an unpleasant visit with his in-laws, but he can't come right out and say it for fear of hurting Ruth. At the same time, Ruth is frustrated that Brent won't own up to the real issue.

It's likely that every married couple has experienced this kind of tension. Your communication sounds good on the surface, but you sense that your spouse is avoiding the key issue. As with Brent, sometimes two different messages are being sent simultaneously: spoken and unspoken. Which one do we usually believe? That's right, the unspoken message. We often try to say something without stating it directly, and just as often the real message gets lost in the verbiage. So a key principle for communication and resolving conflicts is to seek to understand the underlying issue with your spouse.

When you sense that your spouse is not owning up to the real issue, you have three options.

First, you can cave in and ignore the issue along with your spouse. For example, Ruth could say, "Brent, if you go to my parents' for dinner just this one time, I'll never ask you again." Gary and I refer to this as the "back-door" approach. Ruth is going to wheedle and sweet-talk Brent to get her way while avoiding his real reason for staying home. The longer you avoid dealing with the main issue, the longer you will suffer the hurt and anger of the conflict.

Second, you may be tempted to throw your weight around. "Brent, we always do what you want. But the world doesn't revolve around you. We're going to my parents' for dinner, and that's final." But an aggressive approach might touch off a full-blown conflict that will only make things worse.

Third, you can open the door to healing by lovingly confronting the buried issue. Ruth could begin, "Brent, I know you have yard work to do, and I appreciate the way you take care of the yard.

But I also need to spend time with my parents. Do you think you may be avoiding them because of the conflicts in their home?" Using this kind but assertive approach, Ruth could affirm Brent, state her need, and challenge Brent's motives.

In reality, this is exactly what Ruth did. Brent responded, "Ruth, you're right. I do avoid going to see your parents. When I'm there, I'm uncomfortable." As he responded candidly and transparently, Ruth became less defensive. They communicated effectively and eventually reached a resolution.

Here's what Brent and Ruth came up with. They decided to go to dinner, but for only two hours instead of the usual four. They also respectfully confronted Ruth's parents about their constant bickering. Her father was defensive at first, but as Ruth and Brent affirmed their love for her parents, her dad responded more positively. Her mom had suspected that there was an underlying issue when Brent and Ruth visited, so she was relieved when it all came out. Not only are Brent and Ruth relating much better to each other, but their visit also cleared the air for everyone.

Your spouse will probably appreciate your willingness to dig a little deeper to deal with any issues lying beneath the surface of communication. Such honesty is healthy for both of you. There may be some defensiveness because confrontation often creates anxiety. But being direct in communication will help you resolve conflict and avoid additional conflict.

Resolving conflicts occurs more readily when there is a mutual commitment to honest communication in your marriage. Communication facilitates addressing each offense and hurt. In the next chapter we will coach you on the specific skills you will need to confront your conflicts.

11

Confront Your Conflicts

Dan and Marcy had been dating for eleven years and were planning to be married in just a few weeks. The couple came to me for premarital counseling. After we got past the "fear of commitment" issues, we got into the area of communication. I was presenting a number of important topics for couples entering marriage.

Working my way through the process, I asked, "When you two have a conflict, how do you handle it? Do you blow up at each other? Do you pull away from each other and isolate?"

"We've never had a conflict, Dr. Rosberg," Dan said. As he spoke, Marcy nodded in agreement.

I assumed they didn't understand my question. So I rephrased it, pointedly asking what they do when they disagree over something.

"Doctor, we don't fight or disagree," Dan reiterated. "We have never had a conflict, have we, honey?" He flashed Marcy one of those cute little looks only an engaged guy could come up with.

Marcy squished up her face with delight, giving Dan a little squeeze on the arm. "That's right, honey, never," she cooed.

Now, as a professional counselor, I am trained not to display much reaction to what people tell me. But I couldn't prevent my jaw from dropping toward the floor. "You mean you two have never had a disagreement? Never a fight? You've never been ticked with each other?" If I'd had a stethoscope handy, I might have checked each of them for a heartbeat.

"Never," they affirmed emphatically.

"Well, this is a first for me!" I exclaimed in disbelief. "So I guess we'll just move on to the next topic." I checked my notes and continued. "One of the adjustments newly married couples must make is determining how to spend holidays. Thanksgiving is coming up in a couple of weeks. Where will the two of you be spending the day?"

The question had no sooner passed my lips when Dan and Marcy said in unison, "My parents' house!" As they said it, they turned to each with a kind of uh-oh look on their faces.

"All right!" I said, clapping my hands. "I guess we can go back to that last section, because now we have a conflict!"

Dan, Marcy, and I have laughed together about that episode many times since then. They not only worked through their "first" conflict, they have worked through many, and their marriage is doing well today.

Conflicts are a given in every marriage. At some point in every conflict, you and your spouse must confront the issue head-on and resolve it. Having prepared your heart, diffused your anger, and sharpened your communication skills, you need to take the necessary steps to confront the conflict and heal the wounds. (See diagram in figure 11.) We're not talking about going to the mat with your spouse to see who wins. We're talking about the two of you coming together to confront the issues that prompted the offense, hurt, and anger.

Barb will start us off with several tips for confronting your conflicts.

DISARM THE CONFLICT THROUGH PRAYER

Any conflict between you and your spouse is potentially explosive. The combination of wrongs, hurts, and a variety of emotions can touch off a firestorm of cutting words and divisive actions. The first step toward confronting your conflicts is to disarm the potential for further hurt. This can happen only through prayer.

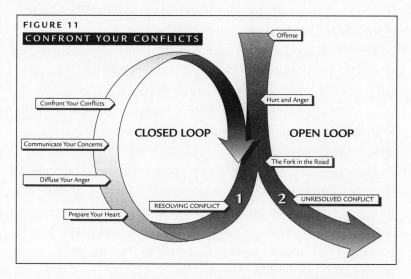

FIGURE 11
CONFRONT YOUR CONFLICTS

Offense

Confront Your Conflicts

Hurt and Anger

CLOSED LOOP   OPEN LOOP

Communicate Your Concerns

The Fork in the Road

Diffuse Your Anger

RESOLVING CONFLICT   1   2   UNRESOLVED CONFLICT

Prepare Your Heart

Gary and I are most effective at resolving a conflict when we have both approached it with tender and respectful spirits. It's the kind of spirit that genuinely wants to work it out with God and with each other. So when we are ready to confront a conflict, one of us will say, "Let's pray together first." Here we are, armed for battle with an arsenal of verbal and emotional weapons at the ready. But we are determined that our marriage is going to glorify Jesus Christ. So we pray and invite Jesus into the process. Talk about draining the anger and fight out of a conflict! Prayer not only controls the flames of conflict, but also forces us to humble ourselves before God and one another. By praying, we admit that neither of us has all the answers and that we must rely on God's wisdom and direction.

The apostle Paul strongly encourages prayer in Colossians 4:2: "Devote yourselves to prayer with an alert mind and a thankful heart." Having an alert mind means being cautious and teachable. Having a thankful heart means recognizing not only God's gift of healing for our hearts but acknowledging God as the healer. Amazing things happen when we bring prayer into a confrontation. God starts to bring restoration to our conflicts. He is glorified, and we begin to experience healing.

Do we always *feel* like praying in the midst of a conflict? No way. Our pride tries to convince us that we can find a solution without God. Indeed, we fear that if we ask God into the discussion, we won't get the justice or revenge we seek. The only way to deflate that pride is to humble ourselves before God and approach the conflict in prayer.

How should you pray as you prepare to confront a conflict? Here is a simple prayer you can use: "Lord Jesus, you alone can soften our hearts and be the center of our discussion so we will not be selfish in our anger and frustration. Help us to resolve our conflict. We place this issue before you, and we ask that you will restore our relationship. Amen."

Prayer not only opens the door to resolutions that are pleasing to God, but also demonstrates to your spouse that you are committed to working it out in a godly way. Prayer can also shorten the length of your discussion and help you reach a solution more quickly.

TAKE ONE ISSUE AT A TIME

Many attempts at resolving marital conflict unfold something like this. Husband and wife are trying to deal with a problem, and then one of them drags out another unresolved issue of pain from the past. In self-defense, the partner under attack responds in kind, digging up another long-buried issue and tossing it into the mix. Before long the initial discussion is buried under a truckload of conflicts dating back to the beginning of the relationship, and nothing gets resolved. The exchange might sound something like this.

"Mike, you never take me anywhere," Val complains.

"Never take you anywhere, huh?" Mike grouses. "We could have gone out last night, except you left me with kitchen cleanup while you watched TV."

"Well, your dad helps your mom in the kitchen all the time," Val comments. "Besides, you never pick up a dish towel unless I ask you to."

"Quit nagging me," Mike says, "I was really ticked off Saturday night when you criticized my driving in front of our friends."

And that's how the discussion continues. Each complaint is answered by another, fanning the flame of conflict into a raging blaze. Piling one offense on another like this can seriously harm the relationship. It is important to concentrate on one issue at a time and get it resolved before moving on to another one.

Gary and I have learned a great way to deal with multiple conflict issues. When a second topic comes up during the discussion, whoever recognizes it first will say, "It seems that we now have two open loops on the table. Let's close the first one and then come back and close the other loop, okay?"

As Mike and Val learned, it is also important to allow one person to talk at a time, without interruption, while the other tunes in for the intended message. Two people can't talk at the same time and still be heard. Furthermore, the tone of the message is vital to the success of closing the loop. As Proverbs 12:18 states, "Some people make cutting remarks, but the words of the wise bring healing."

DEPERSONALIZE THE PROBLEM

Another technique Gary and I use in confronting conflicts is to depersonalize our conflicts. The key to depersonalizing a conflict is to attack the problem without attacking each other.

Marriage researcher John Gottman reports that when four elements are present in your arguments as husband and wife, you may be spiraling downward to an ultimate divorce. When a pattern of *criticism* leads to *defensiveness, contempt,* and ultimately *withdrawal,* Gottman can predict divorce with over 90 percent accuracy.[1] In order to confront your conflicts effectively, you need to approach each other without criticism.

Criticism is different from complaining. It is sometimes appropriate to complain about something your mate says or does. Complaining sounds like this:

- ❋ "It really bugs me when you leave the toilet seat up, Jim. Please be considerate and put the seat down after you use the toilet."
- ❋ "Marian, this is the second time this week you have been late picking up the kids after school. If you think you're going to be late, just let me know so I can help out."

Criticism is an attack on the person instead of the problem. Criticism sounds like this:

- ❋ "All you care about is yourself, Jim. If you had any sense at all you would think about others, and put the toilet seat down."
- ❋ "You blew it again, Marian. I can't believe you don't call when you are running late. You are thoughtless and irresponsible."

One of the most frequent mistakes Gary and I made in the early years of our marriage was being critical of each other. As a result, even when the conflict was over and things had cooled down, we often felt we had added fuel to the fire because of our critical outbursts. One specific incident became a turning point for how we approached our conflicts. It was an insight God gave to Gary, so I'll let him tell you about it.

One day, in the midst of a conflict with Barb, I was feeling exasperated and wanted badly to blame her for what was wrong. I suddenly realized that the real point of my frustration was not Barb but one of her behaviors. Then the phrase we now share with thousands of couples crossed my mind: my spouse is not my enemy. I took a throw pillow off the sofa, tossed it on the floor between us, and said, "Barb, that pillow represents our problem. You are not the problem, and I am not the problem. You are not my enemy; we are on the same team. That pillow is the problem. Let's work together to resolve it."

It was as if a huge lightbulb flashed on for both of us: We needed to depersonalize the issues so we could team up and solve them instead of hammering away at each other's sensitive spirits. I have used this technique in my counseling office ever since. It has done more to help couples deal with problems than any other technique. We spend a lot of time throwing pillows on the floor. It works. Try it!

Barb has one more tip to share before I conclude the chapter.

TAKE A GENTLE APPROACH

Another way to depersonalize the conflict and neutralize the weapons of verbal accusation is to use I-statements instead of you-statements. As illustrated below, you-statements tend to point the finger of accusation at your spouse, and they are often used in an effort to win the argument.

* "Why do you keep criticizing my weight?"
* "You shouldn't get so uptight about your father."
* "You are blowing this problem way out of proportion."

❋ "If you would only do the finances my way, things wouldn't be so bad."

❋ "You make me so mad I could scream."

How would you feel if your spouse shook a finger in your face and said, "You are acting like a real jerk!"? Probably defensive, ready to fight, rejected, or unloved. Do those feelings encourage you to work through the conflict, or do they make you want to fight back or give up? You-statements almost never encourage conflict resolution and often thwart it. Notice how the I-statements take the accusatory sting out of the same issues illustrated above.

❋ "I feel discouraged when my weight problem becomes the topic of our discussion so often."

❋ "Is there anything I can do to help you work through your anger toward your dad?"

❋ "I think there is a more realistic way to view this problem."

❋ "I feel unimportant when you don't ask for my input on how to do the finances."

❋ "I am very angry right now."

Another way to incorporate gentleness when you confront your conflicts is to avoid exaggerations like *always* and *never*. Exaggerated you-statements only add fuel to a conflict. Such overgeneralizations prompt the listener to take a defensive posture, which is not conducive to conflict resolution. For example, let's say you think your spouse is not doing a good job of balancing the checkbook. And last week he or she forgot to transfer some money from savings and bounced a couple of checks. How would your spouse feel if you came at him or her with, "You *always* overwrite on our checkbook"? Your spouse would likely react defensively: "What do you mean *always*? It happened only twice. That's not fair!"

This is where I-messages can help: "I get frustrated when we overdraw our checking account. We need to stay within our balance. How can I help with this?" Now you are working on the conflict together instead of trying to decide a winner and loser. By shifting the approach from "you" to "I," we avoid making the other person the focus of the conflict and are better able to deal with the issues.

Gary will now address another tip for confronting your conflicts, a tip that is particularly applicable to men.

SEEK TO RESOLVE INSTEAD OF REPAIR

I'm not much of a handyman around the house—ask Barb and our two daughters. I remember taking thirteen-year-old Sarah to buy a new bike. As we looked at one particular model, the salesman tried to explain how simple it was to remove the front wheel. He did it with ease, then said, "Okay, Gary, do you know how to do it now?"

Sarah rolled her eyes, knowing me to be a real klutz at such things. I just stared at the wheel and said, "Mike, you know me. I'm a counselor, not a mechanic."

But when it comes to resolving conflict at home, I'm like a lot of other men. My first response is to jump in and try to fix the problem by righting the wrong or changing someone else's behavior. But a quick-fix approach can get you into real trouble because your spouse may think you are trying to fix him or her. Sometimes your spouse just needs you to listen, empathize, provide support, or demonstrate that you care.

So what should you do when you don't know what to do in a conflict? Simply ask your spouse what he or she needs from you. Our friends Charles and Janet shared with us a healthy alternative to "fixing" a conflict. Janet's father was an engineer—a problem-solver by trade. When she was growing up, Janet and her father had their share of conflicts, and her dad's solution was to try to fix them, which led to further breakdowns in their communication.

Realizing that his approach wasn't working, Janet's dad took another tack. Instead of pummeling Janet with solutions, he would say in the midst of a meltdown, "Janet, I love you deeply, and I don't want to blow it with you. What do you need from me right now: sympathy or a solution?" It worked every time. And when Janet married Charles, he was wise enough to continue using this excellent technique in their marriage.

Barb and I have employed this technique in our marriage. Often when she comes to me with a problem or a conflict, I will ask point-blank, "What do you need from me: sympathy or a solution?" We recommend this approach to you. Your spouse's answer to that simple question will probably save you a lot of guesswork and wasted effort.

WORK TOWARD A DECISION

In many conflicts, resolution is not achieved until the two of you make a decision about what needs to happen. Some conflicts may not need a decision because airing out the issues and providing empathy may take care of it. But as you confront your conflicts, realize that you will likely come to the point where you need to change course in some way, as a couple or as individuals.

Barb came to me once and said, "Gary, I think you're overcommitted again. So many people want a piece of you, and sometimes there isn't much left over for us at home."

Her words hit me like a sledgehammer—and she was right. I needed to hear it. I had overcommitted to counseling appointments and speaking engagements, and the two were on a collision course with my home life. It tends to be a recurring source of conflict between us. I get so busy helping others and feeding my own need to minister that I rob Barb of my time and attention.

So we talked it out. I listened to Barb's frustration over my frantic schedule. She is my partner in ministry, and as much as she supports me, she is also the most effective person I know at expressing her needs. Barb also listened as I voiced my frustration at not being able to do everything I felt called to do. We prayed together and sought God's direction. We talked about whether I was always responding to God's call for my life or whether my own "call" got mixed up in there somewhere. We validated each other's hurts and frustrations.

It felt great to get everything out on the table. We listened to each other, and we empathized. But that wasn't enough. In this case, we needed to take another important step toward closing the loop. We needed to make some changes in my weekly schedule. So we weighed the options and reached a mutually satisfying decision.

As you confront your conflicts, be aware that some decisions may be necessary. When you come to the decision-making stage, the first questions to ask each other are, "What does the Bible say about this situation? Is there a clear admonition we need to obey?" How's that for getting to the heart of the matter? It's not, "What do we feel like doing?" or "What do other people think we ought to do?" Those may be good questions, but they are secondary to what God has to say. Put God's principles on the table immediately so you can fall in line with them. You need to elevate the Bible above your other options in making decisions.

Sometimes the Bible does not give specific direction about an issue. For example, you and your spouse are arguing over whether to send your children to public school or a private Christian school. Try as you might, you won't find a "thus says the Lord" that will make that decision for you. At these times, you need to seek God's wisdom for making the best decision in that situation. Here are a couple of suggestions that will help you reach your decisions and resolve your conflicts.

Stay open to different options. Avoid tunnel vision as you make your decisions. Think through all the possibilities instead of jumping on the first one—or the only one—you see. Brainstorm about different options with your spouse. Invite trusted family members or friends to share their wisdom on the issue. You can get so locked into "the way we've always done it" that you fail to recognize or appreciate a better solution.

Once you have a few workable ideas, you can always "test drive" one to see if it works. The best approach is to go with your best option but remain open to changing if that option doesn't prove to be the best.

Barb and I talked through a number of options for cutting back on my counseling schedule. We decided that with our radio and speaking schedules increasing, we needed to diminish my counseling appointments commensurately. I had been increasing both, and that was the cause of the conflict.

Be open to not doing it your way. How would you react if your spouse said something like, "You know, honey, your idea is just as good as mine, if not better. Why don't we try doing it your way"? If your spouse tends to be a controller, no other statement would cause you more shock! That's a great way to resolve conflict, but it rarely happens so easily. Instead, we instinctively want to resolve things according to what we think is best.

One of the most important aspects of resolving conflict is to defer to your spouse whenever possible, helping your spouse realize that he or she is more important than the issue at hand. This is essentially what the apostle Paul meant when he wrote, "So encourage each other and build each other up, just as you are already doing" (1 Thessalonians 5:11). We are to edify and encourage each other as husband and wife, delighting in the opportunity to resolve a conflict to our spouse's advantage. This may mean swallowing your pride and relinquishing control. But when each of you is committed to edifying and encouraging the other, the rewards will be well worth the sacrifice.

We encourage you as a couple to take a head-on approach to confronting your conflicts in a way that will honor your spouse above all else. This honest, direct, and caring style will incorporate your thoughts, feelings, and needs on the decision-making part of conflict resolution. As that occurs, you are ready for the next stage of healing your relationship. This stage is the most difficult for many couples, yet it brings the greatest amount of healing. It is the process of forgiveness, and it will do more to bring you closer to God and to each other than anything else you can do.

12

Forgive Your Spouse

The following story is based on real events in the life of a real couple. The names have been changed and the details slightly fictionalized to protect their privacy. But Gary and I believe the serious conflict this couple experienced illustrates the importance of forgiveness in closing the loop.

The phone was ringing as Katy walked into the house after work. The readout displayed her husband's name and cell phone number. Walker had just left for another of his frequent business trips this morning. Katy was surprised to hear from him so soon because he usually didn't call until late in the evening.

She picked up and said hello, but there was no response. She could hear background voices, so she said hello again. No one returned her greeting. She listened carefully. One of the faint voices she could hear was Walker's. Katy smiled, realizing that her husband must have jostled his cell phone, tapping the speed-dial button and calling home without realizing it. The phone was probably in his suit jacket or in his briefcase.

Curious about what Walker was doing, Katy decided to "eavesdrop" for a few seconds. There were traffic noises in the background. Katy assumed Walker was in the rental car on his way to dinner with his clients. Listening closer, she could hear only one other voice, a woman's voice. It sounded familiar, but she couldn't place it.

Then she began to pick up on the conversation. Her breath caught in her throat. The exchange between Walker and the woman was personal, even intimate. They were talking about making love . . . with each other. Katy stiffened and bit her lip. There was no doubt about what was going on. Reality doubled her over like a vicious blow to the stomach. Her husband was having an affair.

Katy had never imagined the possibility that Walker might be unfaithful to her. They were both new Christians. Their old life—which had included many shameful behaviors—was behind them. Or so Katy thought. Then she recognized the woman's voice. It was Nan, Walker's administrative assistant. Nan was also married, and the two couples had gone out for dinner together on occasion. The fact that Walker was involved with Nan, someone Katy knew and liked, made the discovery even worse. Stunned and heartsick, Katy quietly hung up the phone.

When Walker returned home from his trip two days later, Katy angrily confronted him with what she had heard over the phone. Exposed and ashamed, Walker admitted that he and Nan had been carrying on an affair for several weeks, secretly sharing a hotel room on their many business trips together. He apologized for hurting her and affirmed his love for Katy. He promised to break off the relationship and make sure Nan was released from the company. When he asked Katy to forgive him, she replied, "I don't think I can, Walker. What's more, right now I don't even want to."

A few days later, Walker confessed his secret life to his weekly men's Bible study group. He was broken and repentant. He asked the guys to forgive him for living a lie. And he asked them to pray that Katy would someday forgive him.

We hope you and your spouse never experience the depth of offense and hurt that Katy and Walker did. But no matter how you have hurt one another, forgiveness is the key step to closing every loop of conflict in your marriage. Forgiveness is the core of forgiving love. Whether you are feeling the sting of an unkind remark or the sledgehammer blow of infidelity, without forgiveness, you will be trapped in your pain and anger. Without forgiveness, you will never experience the peace of reconciliation and the joy of restoration in your marriage.

It is important to recognize that closing the loop of offense with forgiveness comes only after the expression of the emotions of hurt and anger. It doesn't occur until heart preparation takes place and the lines of communication are open. Biblical forgiveness happens best in the context of the steps for closing the loop presented in the previous chapters. (See diagram in figure 12.)

In this chapter, I will share with you what true, biblical forgiveness is and is *not*. Then Gary will coach you through the necessary steps for seeking and granting forgiveness in your marriage relationship.

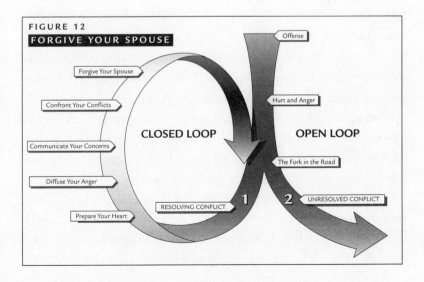

FIGURE 12
FORGIVE YOUR SPOUSE

Forgive Your Spouse

Confront Your Conflicts

Communicate Your Concerns

Diffuse Your Anger

Prepare Your Heart

CLOSED LOOP

OPEN LOOP

Offense

Hurt and Anger

The Fork in the Road

RESOLVING CONFLICT 1

2 UNRESOLVED CONFLICT

WHAT FORGIVENESS LOOKS LIKE

That phone call from Walker—the one he didn't intend to make—devastated Katy. She felt betrayed, devastated, broken-hearted. Walker's infidelity was worse than a dagger plunged into her heart. Her love for him had sustained a mortal wound. She wondered if she would ever recover—or if it was even worth trying. At first she saw only one way out: divorce.

Perhaps you have felt the dagger of betrayal and unfaithfulness slash into your heart. More than likely, the offenses you have suffered are not as traumatic or life-threatening to your marriage. But they still cut and wound and hurt. Healing and restoration come through biblical forgiveness. The following elements give us a clear picture of what God's brand of forgiveness in a relationship looks like.

Forgiveness Acknowledges the Hurt

Some people think that forgiveness means pretending that the offense didn't hurt, or at least didn't hurt very badly. They may rationalize that their spouses' actions were unintentional and that their pain is irrational. Others refuse to acknowledge the hurt because they are unwilling to give their spouses the satisfaction of knowing the offense hit the mark. Still others keep quiet about the hurt because they fear their transparency will give their spouses the ammunition to hurt them again.

Failing to acknowledge the pain of your spouse's offense is like suffering with a toothache but refusing to go to the dentist. The hurt cannot be healed until you admit it's there. First, we must admit to ourselves that we were hurt. Second, we must acknowledge our hurt and pain to God. Jesus invites us, "Come to me, all of you who are weary and carry heavy burdens, and I will give you rest" (Matthew 11:28). The apostle Peter instructs, "Give all your worries and cares to God, for he cares about what happens to you" (1 Peter 5:7). And third, we must acknowledge to our spouse that the offense hurt. Being up front about your pain may be just the impetus your spouse needs to work toward healing.

Katy was very aware of her pain. During the confrontation, she let Walker have it with both barrels, declaring in no uncertain terms that his unfaithfulness had wounded her deeply, perhaps irreparably. By acknowledging that she was hurt, Katy was in position to exercise forgiveness.

Forgiveness Releases the Offense and the Offender

When you drive a big sliver into your finger, you don't protect the sliver to keep it from falling out. Rather, you hurry for the tweezers and remove it. If you don't get the sliver out right away and sanitize the wound, you risk infection.

Similarly, when you are wounded by your spouse's offense, it is important to let it go. It will take some time to get to the point of releasing the offense and the offender. Questions need to be asked and answered honestly. Emotions need to be experienced and expressed honestly. You may lose some sleep and miss some meals in the process. Distractions will abound. Yet, in time, you need to let it go. Does your offending spouse deserve it? Maybe not. Is it easy? No, it is gut-wrenching. Do we let it go perfectly? No, there are relapses. But if you don't consciously release your spouse from the offense, the pain only mounts.

Releasing your spouse means choosing *not* to punish him or her, *not* to seek revenge—either openly or secretly—and *not* to exact retribution for what he or she did. By deciding to release your spouse from the offense, you are following God's example of forgiveness. The apostle Paul explained, "God was in Christ, reconciling the world to himself, no longer counting people's sins against them" (2 Corinthians 5:19).

Jesus calls us to be forgiving people. He illustrated this principle in the parable of the unmerciful servant, found in Matthew 18. Jesus described a servant who owed millions of dollars to the king, who mercifully forgave the servant's enormous debt. But the forgiven servant turned around and pressured a fellow servant to pay the few dollars he owed him. When the man couldn't pay, the hard-hearted servant threw him into prison.

When the king heard what had happened, he had the unforgiving servant thrown into prison as well. Jesus concluded, "That's what my heavenly Father will do to you if you refuse to forgive your brothers and sisters in your heart" (Matthew 18:35). When Jesus says "forgive your brothers and sisters," we understand that he is talking about being a forgiving person in all our human relationships, and your marriage is at the top of the list.

Katy has struggled with this element of forgiveness. Walker has followed through with the repentance he promised. Nan is out of his life for good, and Walker has done everything he knows to do to prove his love to Katy. Things will go well for a few weeks, then Katy's temptation to remind him of what he has done often surfaces, and she drags out his sin and uses it against him. She won't let it go, and her reluctance has stopped the restoration of their marriage dead in its tracks. As counselors, we understand the deep pain she experiences. Yet we also know that until she releases Walker to God, all efforts at restoration will be sabotaged.

You will receive a tremendous payoff when you let your spouse off the hook, and both you and your spouse are the beneficiaries. In his excellent book *Forgive and Forget,* psychologist Lewis Smedes wrote, "When you release the wrongdoer from the wrong, you cut a malignant tumor out of your inner life. You set a prisoner free, but you discover that the real prisoner was yourself."[1] Failure to let go of your spouse's offense will hurt you as much as it will hurt your spouse.

Forgiveness Relinquishes Resentment

Relinquishing resentment is part of letting your spouse off the hook. Resentment is an internal monster that roars hateful suggestions like, "Get back at him" or "Don't ever forget what she did to you" or "He doesn't deserve your forgiveness" or "She'll never change." Resentment is a large part of Katy's difficulty in letting Walker off the hook for his affair. Whenever Walker makes some positive steps in their relationship, instead of drawing nearer to him, Katy thinks about his betrayal and backs away. In order to let go of the offense, you must let go of the resentment.

Gary and I can't think of a better example of relinquishing resentment than Joseph in the Old Testament. Genesis 37–50 tells how Joseph's jealous brothers cruelly sold him into slavery. God used that act of evil for good, however, and eventually placed Joseph in a position of power in Egypt.

Joseph's brothers later traveled to Egypt during a famine, seeking to buy food. They came to Joseph, not knowing who he was. But Joseph recognized them, and he could have paid them back big-time for what they did to him. But he had long since released his brothers from their offense and relinquished any resentment he may have felt. So he sincerely forgave them and made provision for a safe and secure life for all of them.

Resentment feeds anger and keeps the loop open. It impairs our sense of understanding, undermines the healing of our hearts, and destroys the working of a gracious God in our lives.

Forgiveness Is an Act of Grace

Katy and Walker have been going through the same cycle repeatedly for over two years now. Walker assures her of his love and renewed commitment to be faithful. They draw closer together, encouraging Walker to think that she has given up her thoughts of divorce. Then something reminds Katy of what he did, twisting the dagger of pain in her heart. She pulls back again, saying things like, "I just can't get over it. What an awful thing you did. Maybe I just ought to leave."

Walker then goes through his familiar monologue: "Katy, I freely admit that what I did was wrong. I'm guilty, and there's no way I can undo it or pay you back for the hurt I caused you. I know that your pain is a consequence of my sin. I have asked God to forgive me, and he has. I'm begging you to forgive me too."

For a few weeks their life is fairly normal, then the cycle starts up again. No matter what he does, Walker cannot convince Katy to just forgive him. So far, she hasn't been able to look past his offense and just say, "I forgive you."

Forgiveness is essentially an act of grace, a gift of love. You can't work for grace. You can't jump through the right hoops to earn it. You can't perfect your performance in order to deserve it. Grace is simply a gift.

The Bible instructs us, "Be kind to each other, tenderhearted, forgiving one another, just as God through Christ has forgiven you" (Ephesians 4:32). How did God forgive us? Did we earn it? Did Jesus die on the cross because we achieved something to merit such a sacrifice? No, God's forgiveness is a gift of grace. And that's how God expects us to forgive our spouses and others—not because they have earned enough points through good behavior, but because we choose to give it as a gift. Theologian F. F. Bruce wrote, "The free grace of the Father's forgiving love is the pattern for his children in their forgiveness of one another."[2]

Forgiveness means giving your spouse a second chance, not because he or she deserves it, but because you choose to extend grace to your spouse just as God has extended grace to you. Forgiveness also means giving your spouse a third chance, a fourth chance, and so on. The disciple Peter once asked Jesus, "Lord, how often should I forgive someone who sins against me? Seven times?" Jesus replied, "No! . . . seventy times seven!" (Matthew

18:21-22). The reservoir of forgiveness in your marriage should never run dry.

WHAT FORGIVENESS IS NOT: SIX MYTHS ABOUT FORGIVENESS

Propagandists know that if you repeat a lie often enough, people will start to believe it. Hearing the lie so frequently, they assume it must be true. Unfortunately, a few lies about forgiveness—we call them myths—have taken root in society. People believe them because they hear them so often. In order for you to move forward in forgiving love, you must clear these lies out of the way and find the truth behind them.

Myth #1: When I Forgive, I Must Also Forget

How often have you heard someone say, "I know I haven't forgiven him because I haven't forgotten what he did to me"? The idea that you have to forget in order to forgive is a myth. Ethicist Lewis Smedes, author of *Forgive and Forget,* wrote:

> When we forgive someone, we do not forget the hurtful act, as if forgetting came along with the forgiveness package, the way strings come with a violin. Begin with basics. If you forget, you will not forgive at all. You can never forgive people for things you have forgotten about. You need to forgive precisely because you have not forgotten what someone did; your memory keeps the pain alive long after the actual hurt has stopped. Remembering is your storage of pain. It is why you need to be healed in the first place.[3]

Gary and I don't believe God intends for us to forget the pain in our lives. To the contrary, we remember it so we can value the lessons we learn from it. Remembering also helps us keep from repeating some painful mistakes.

When Jill called into our radio program, she was struggling with this issue of forgiveness. She said, "I can't forget what Rich did to me. It plays over and over in my head." She went on to explain how her husband had offended her repeatedly. He was gone from their home fifteen to eighteen hours a day, either working or playing golf. When he was home, he was emotionally absent or hostile. He alienated the children and shut down emotionally with her. Jill and Rich had not sat and talked for months. She felt trapped and was becoming embittered.

"The Bible says God forgives and forgets our sin," Jill said. "But I can't forget, so I must not have forgiven him."

"Yes, God forgives and forgets our sin, Jill. That's the promise of Jeremiah 31:34," Gary said. "But you're not God. You don't have the power to forget as he does." As Jill began to internalize that forgiving is separate from forgetting, she gained hope that she could resolve the pain of her heart.

How do we resolve the pain of offenses we can't forget? You start by admitting to yourself that you don't have to forget. We are called to remember without condemnation. The apostle Paul wrote, "So now there is no condemnation for those who belong to Christ Jesus" (Romans 8:1). God has forgiven our sin and no longer condemns us. We must forgive our spouses in the same way even when we cannot forget the offense. As you do, you can ask God to ease your pain. This takes you off the hook of trying to make yourself forget that your spouse wounded you.

Your pain will also diminish as you focus on the more positive, joyful aspects of your marriage. God can help you generate fresh memories that will push the bad memories into the background and help you renew your relationship.

It is also important for you to grow in your relationship with Jesus, seeking him for instruction and comfort in your pain. Ask yourself: What is God teaching me through these difficult times? Am I finding the balance between dealing with my painful memories and seeking positive interaction with my spouse?

Myth #2: The Hurt Is Too Great; It Is Impossible for Me to Forgive

Have you ever been hurt so deeply in your marriage that you were sure you could never forgive? Katy has been stuck on this myth for a couple of years. Gary and I talk with many other women—and even some men—who are so deeply hurt and angry over their spouse's infidelity, cruelty, or abuse that forgiveness seems as impossible as climbing Mount Everest barefoot. And like Katy, they don't even *want* to forgive at that point.

Forgiveness may be difficult, but it is never impossible in God's strength. God would never ask you to do something you cannot do. Even when the last thing you want to do—or think you can do—is forgive your spouse, God can help you do it. In fact, the more impossible forgiveness seems to you, the more you need to lean on Jesus for his peace, compassion, and strength. As you do, God will help you release your spouse from the offense and begin to heal your deep hurt.

Myth #3: I Don't Feel Like Forgiving, So My Forgiveness Can't Be Genuine

Gary and I help husbands and wives work through forgiveness during our conferences around the country and on our daily radio program. Yet even after all we have learned and taught about forgiveness, whenever we are in conflict, neither of us really feels like forgiving the other. But forgiveness isn't about feelings. Forgiving your spouse is a choice, an act of the will. If you wait to forgive until you feel like it, you will likely never forgive. Feelings are antecedents of thoughts. Feelings can't think; they can only feel, and they cannot be trusted as the main element in deciding to forgive. Forgiveness is the right thing to do, whether you are emotionally moved to do so or not. If you wait for a feeling, you are giving more opportunity for resentment and bitterness to fester in your heart.

The willful decision to forgive supersedes your feelings, but it doesn't deny them. It's okay to admit that you are hurt, angry, or disappointed and still say, "I forgive you." And when you don't feel like forgiving, you need to ask God for the strength to enter the process anyway. He will empower you to forgive if you honestly seek him.

Myth #4: I Can't Forgive until My Spouse Asks for It

We are often asked, "What if my spouse won't discuss the issue with me and doesn't want to close the loop? Can I still forgive him or her?" Yes, even though you cannot make your spouse do what he or she should do, you can still follow through with your part of the process. The apostle Paul wrote, "Do your part to live in peace with everyone, as much as possible" (Romans 12:18).

Should you still try to encourage your spouse toward forgiveness and restoration? Certainly. If there is significant hurt, it may be easy for you to use your spouse's resistance as an excuse to shelve the idea of closing the loop. But even if your spouse's unwillingness makes the process more difficult, you can still forge on, making your intentions clear and remaining open to discussion on the issues. In the meantime, pray that God will give you insight and direction for relating to your spouse in this conflict.

Myth #5: In Order to Forgive, I Must Pretend That Nothing Bad Happened

Some people try to minimize or deny their spouse's offense, hoping it will allow them to forgive. That's not a good idea! Forgiveness is not an exercise in trying to make an offense disappear. On the contrary, granting forgiveness requires us to confront the reality that something painful *did* happen. If nothing happened, there would be nothing to forgive. Trying to make less of the offense only makes the freedom of forgiveness more elusive.

Furthermore, true forgiveness doesn't pretend that the offense didn't hurt. Rather, true forgiveness acknowledges what really happened and how badly it hurt; then it chooses to let go of the offense. Forgiveness says, "I know what you did, and it really hurt. But I choose to forgive you anyway."

In fact, Gary and I recommend that couples revisit the hurt periodically during the healing process. It may sound illogical to dredge up old wounds while you are trying to heal. But that offense is part of your history, and you can't avoid talking about it as if it didn't happen. Review the issue occasionally, and encourage each other with what God has taught you. It may be painful to do, but this activity can assist the healing process.

Another problem people have with forgiveness is assuming that it automatically restores trust in their spouse after the offense. Taken to the extreme, this false view would mean that Katy should forgive Walker for his unfaithfulness and then encourage him to go on another business trip with Nan. But forgiveness and trust are two different concepts. Forgiveness is a gift, freely bestowed. Trust needs to be earned. You may forgive your spouse for his or her offense in some area, but it may take some time to trust your spouse in that area again.

Rebuilding trust is such an important part of closing the loop that we have devoted the final chapter to the topic.

Myth #6: I Must Forgive Right Away, Or It Doesn't Count
Yes, Ephesians 4:26 admonishes, "Don't let the sun go down while you are still angry." But Gary and I don't believe this Bible verse is a formula for the amount of time it should take to grant forgiveness. The Bible does instruct us to restore a broken relationship with our spouse and makes it clear that we should not let

anger fester in our hearts. Forgiveness, however, is an act of the will, and it may take some time to reach the point where you are able to grant it. Hurrying to forgive as if you are on a time limit results in what we call "cheap forgiveness." It's not genuine, and it hinders real healing.

Remember: Granting forgiveness is a process. You need to prepare your heart, deal with your anger, and talk through the conflict and offense with your spouse. Then you need to walk through the steps of forgiveness, which Gary will outline in the next section. All of this takes time. If the offense is minor, the forgiveness process may take less time. But if the offense is major, such as the major conflict between Katy and Walker, you need to be prepared for a longer process. The mistake is in refusing to begin the process.

HOW FORGIVENESS HAPPENS: SIX ELEMENTS OF WHOLE FORGIVENESS

Who is supposed to initiate the process of forgiveness in a marriage relationship: the offender or the offended? Barb and I don't think it really matters. Both of you are responsible for clearing up conflicts by initiating forgiveness. If your spouse offends you and you refuse to resolve the conflict until he or she makes the first move, you could be waiting a long time. And if your spouse plays by the same rules, think of all the intimacy you could forfeit by waiting each other out.

Barb and I mutually accept the role of being peacemakers in our marriage. Ideally, whoever recognizes the conflict first is the one to bring it up and initiate forgiveness regardless of who is at fault. If one of us senses friction, that person usually confronts the other on the issue. I use the words "ideally" and "usually" because, just like at your house, Barb and I are sometimes deterred from initiating forgiveness by hurt, anger, or pride. That's why it is important to share the responsibility equally. Since both of us are committed to peace, if one is a little slow to step up, the other is there to take up the slack. This virtually assures that the conflict will be resolved sooner rather than later.

We call this process "whole forgiveness." In any offense, someone offends and someone is offended. Of course, it's rarely that cut-and-dried. In many conflicts, you both offend each other to some degree. For example, your spouse hurts you with a critical remark, so you snap back with a zinger of your own. Or you forget to buy your spouse a birthday gift, and in return he or she gives you the cold shoulder for two days.

For each offense, whole forgiveness requires action on the part of both the offender and the offended. We have represented this activity with the following six statements for closing the loop with forgiveness:

1. I was wrong.
2. I'm sorry.
3. I don't ever want to hurt you like this again.
4. Will you forgive me?
5. I forgive you and close the loop on this issue.
6. I forgive you for . . .

The first four statements are for *requesting* forgiveness; the last two are for *granting* forgiveness. Over the course of your relationship, you will each have plenty of opportunity with both sides of the process. As you follow these guidelines, not mechanically or out of duty, but sensitively and compassionately, you can experience healing in any conflict, great or small.

Requesting Forgiveness

Statement #1: I was wrong. Let's go back to the major conflict between Katy and Walker. When Katy found out about Walker's affair with Nan, his coworker, she exploded with hurt and anger. Walker was dead wrong for doing what he did. And who knows how long he would have remained secretly involved with Nan if his cell phone had not betrayed him. But once Katy found out, at least Walker did the right thing. He came clean with his wife: "Katy, I was wrong." The element of confession is critical in the process of seeking forgiveness.

The admission of wrongful behavior starts the process of whole forgiveness in motion. It's not very important which partner points out the offense. The approach would have been the same had Walker come to Katy and confessed his affair before she found out. The key is for the offending party to say categorically, "What I did was wrong."

You may be tempted to wriggle off the hook at this stage by stopping short of, "I was wrong." The following statements *sound* like the admission of wrong, but notice how they don't quite go far enough: "OK, if you think I did something wrong, let's talk about it"; "I don't think what I did was such a big deal, but since you think it was, let's talk about it." You need to confront the offense for what it is. Say something like, "I am wrong"; "What I did to you is wrong"; "I have done wrong and need to talk to you about what I did to offend you."

Statement #2: I'm sorry. Simply admitting wrong behavior is insufficient. Having determined the nature of what you said or did, you need to state how you feel about what you said or did. Do you feel regret about hurting your spouse? Certainly you do! You need to express that sorrow. Together, the admission of wrongdoing and the expression of sorrow convey to your spouse your sincerity about making things right.

The apostle Paul understood what it means to express sorrow. He wrote: "Now I am glad I sent it [a letter of correction], not because it hurt you, but because the pain caused you to have remorse and change your ways. It was the kind of sorrow God wants his people to have, so you were not harmed by us in any way. For God can use sorrow in our lives to help us turn away from sin and seek salvation. We will never regret that kind of sorrow. But sorrow without repentance is the kind that results in death" (2 Corinthians 7:9-10).

The expression of remorse and sorrow is healthy when it leads to healing in the relationship with your spouse and with God. It also leads to empathy and a true sense of restoration. Empathy means seeing the issue from your spouse's perspective, walking in his or her shoes, so to speak. Your empathy will diminish the distance between you and your hurting spouse, allowing defensive shields to be lowered so open communication can begin. Your empathy will allow your spouse to feel heard and cared for.

Statement #3: I don't ever want to hurt you like this again. "Katy, I know I hurt you deeply," Walker said during his confession. "I could see the pain in your eyes as you told me what you heard on the cell phone. I can't tell you how sad I am about how I hurt you. I never want to cause you such pain again."

Walker made two important admissions in this statement. First, he acknowledged the hurt he had caused his wife. Seeing her deep hurt caused him pain, which he openly admitted. Your spouse needs to know that you feel something of the pain your offense caused him or her.

Second, Walker expressed repentance by declaring his intention not to hurt Katy like that again. Admitting wrong behavior and expressing sorrow without indicating a desire to change leaves forgiveness incomplete. Your repentance tells your spouse that you desire to turn from your hurtful ways.

True repentance requires a change of heart and mind. It goes beyond "I'm sorry" to actually changing your hurtful behavior and the patterns of your offenses. Seeking forgiveness without promising repentance is pointless. It would be like Walker saying, "I'm sorry I hurt you, Katy. And by the way, next weekend Nan and I are traveling together on business." Only when you commit to turning away from your hurtful behavior can true healing take place.

This is the same response God seeks from us in our sinfulness. When we confess our sin, he graciously forgives (see 1 John 1:9). But he doesn't expect us to keep going in the same sinful direction. He's looking for us to change direction. The apostle Paul challenges believers, "Should we keep on sinning so that God can show us more and more kindness and forgiveness? Of course not! Since we have died to sin, how can we continue to live in it?" (Romans 6:1-2).

God's forgiveness is free and always available, but we cheapen it when we don't walk away from the very behavior for which we seek forgiveness. Similarly, you depreciate the precious gift of your spouse's forgiveness if you fail to stop doing the behavior that hurt him or her.

Statement #4: Will you forgive me? Once Walker confessed his wrong to Katy, expressed his sorrow, and committed to repentance, he had to bring the issue to a head. He had to ask his wife to forgive him for his unfaithfulness. It was one of the most difficult things he has done in his life.

This key question—"Will you forgive me?"—brings the process of whole forgiveness to a crescendo. It is forgiving love at its best, the ultimate in humility and intimacy in marriage. You are never more vulnerable to your spouse than when you make this request. It means putting yourself at his or her feet as a servant to receive an undeserved favor. In asking this question, you are swinging the door wide open for whole forgiveness.

If you omit any of the four elements in requesting forgiveness, you run the risk of leaving the conflict unresolved. Too often we leap to the final element and ask for forgiveness without acknowledging any understanding, remorse, or repentance. This is cheap forgiveness, and it creates uncertainty in your spouse about how to respond. It is very important that you take all four steps as you approach your spouse for forgiveness.

Granting Forgiveness

When your spouse comes seeking your forgiveness, you can participate in whole forgiveness in two ways: graciously and specifically. The last two statements of whole forgiveness will walk you through the process.

Statement #5: I forgive you and close the loop on this issue. When you say, "Yes, I forgive you," you are reflecting the love of a gracious, forgiving God. You are granting something your spouse doesn't deserve. It is a free gift; it cannot be earned or bargained for. It cannot be taken back or returned. There are no strings attached.

This is the point where Katy struggles with granting forgiveness to Walker. She eventually came to the place where she could say, "Okay, I forgive you." But she is still hurting so much that she kind of keeps Walker and his offense on a leash, ready to pull it back if she changes her mind.

That's not genuine forgiveness. When you say, "I forgive you," you must let go of the offense once and for all and set your spouse free. When you do, there is closure. Both you and your spouse experience emotional relief. The pressure is off, the pain begins to subside, and the healing starts.

Some people give the gift of forgiveness with a slap on the back, essentially saying, "Hey, no problem. We all mess up." Others do so with a whispered "Yes" or a quiet nod, a rare moment of closeness when you gaze into your spouse's eyes and sense the oneness growing in your relationship. Barb and I don't think God cares much about your posture or tone of voice. He does care about the sincerity of your heart. When you forgive graciously, your spouse can sense it. It's real—authentic and supernatural. You are well on your way to rebuilding a broken relationship.

Statement #6: I forgive you for . . . In addition to being gracious, your forgiveness needs to be specific. State precisely the offenses for which you are granting forgiveness, the very offenses for which your spouse has requested forgiveness. For example: "I forgive you for not spending more time with me last weekend"; "I forgive you for committing me to serve on a church committee without asking me first"; "I forgive you for backing into the lamppost with my new car." This is another area of struggle for Katy. She just can't bring herself to say, "I forgive you, Walker, for having an affair with Nan."

Being specific assures your spouse how complete your forgiveness is. It doesn't leave anything hanging in the air. It answers for your spouse the nagging question he or she may have: *Did he or she understand what I was asking forgiveness for? Did he or she really forgive me for what I did?*

Reconciliation: The Goal of Whole Forgiveness

The desired result of this sometimes difficult and painful process is to reconcile as husband and wife. You want to get back to where you were before the offense occurred so you can resume moving forward in your relationship. You want to leave the hurt and anger in the dust and press on with building your divorce-proof marriage. Reconciliation can happen only when whole forgiveness happens—forgiveness requested, forgiveness granted.

"But what if my spouse won't request forgiveness for hurting me?" someone may ask. "Or what if my spouse won't grant forgiveness when I request it? Can forgiveness and reconciliation still happen?"

In these cases, forgiveness is partial and incomplete, not whole, and reconciliation is thwarted. You can graciously forgive your spouse for an offense even if he or she doesn't request it. But you cannot be fully reconciled without your spouse's participation. Furthermore, you can humbly confess your wrong and request forgiveness for your offense, but if your spouse does not grant it, again, reconciliation can't happen. As counselors Dr. David Stoop and James Masteller write, "Forgiveness is unilateral. It is something we can do all by ourselves. Reconciliation requires the participation of another person. We cannot 'make it happen,' no matter how hard we try."[4]

Wayne and Samantha are a case in point. After nine years of marriage and two kids, they had drifted apart. Wayne started spending time outside the church with a woman from their Bible study group. Samantha repeatedly asked if anything was going on between the two of them, but Wayne insisted nothing was. As time went on, however, Wayne's relationship with the woman escalated from an emotional affair to a full-blown sexual affair. Both couples separated as a result.

I met Samantha and Wayne at a conference where Barb and I were speaking. Having heard God's design for divorce-proofing marriage, this couple made an appointment to see me at the end of the conference. Samantha looked free and relieved, as if a heavy weight had been lifted from her shoulders. God had ministered to her powerfully during the sessions. Wayne, on the other hand, seemed stuck in the mess he had created with the other woman. Even with all the information he had received on how to restore their marriage, he was not willing to leave his affair.

We talked about their marriage for an hour. But my words bounced off Wayne like a rubber ball off a concrete wall. Just as we were about to leave, Samantha glanced at Wayne and then made an amazing statement: "Gary, no matter what happens to our marriage now, I now know I can forgive him."

"Even if he doesn't come home, Samantha?" I pressed gently.

"Even if he doesn't come home," she affirmed, tears rolling down her cheeks.

Wayne was sorry for what he had done, but he was not ready to quit doing it. Yet somehow Samantha was able to forgive him.

She was still deeply hurt and fearful about the future. But she chose to forgive even though reconciliation seemed unattainable. She had learned that withholding her forgiveness, even though it was not requested, would not only wreck her family but also destroy her personally.

Samantha is a rare person. Katy is not there yet, and until she relinquishes control, she will continue to be bound by her lack of forgiveness. Samantha was able to let Jesus control her life instead of Wayne. She had captured the truth that God would not bail out on her; she could trust him even when her trust in her husband had been decimated. She didn't forgive Wayne because he had asked for it; he hadn't. She forgave Wayne because of who Jesus is and what he had done for her.

Unfortunately, Samantha and Wayne never reconciled. She was willing, but he was not. Reconciliation can occur only when both spouses want it and pursue it through whole forgiveness.

One step remains in the process of choosing to close the loop. You and your spouse need to rebuild any trust that may have been eroded as a result of the offense, hurt, and anger. In the final chapter, Barb and I will show you how to do that.

13

Rebuild Your Trust

Healing the hurt in your marriage involves more than requesting and granting forgiveness when offenses happen between you. Every hurt, great or small, chips away at the mutual trust that is essential in a divorce-proof marriage. Gary and I have learned from our own experience and from countless couples we have dealt with that forgiveness must be followed by an effort to rebuild the trust that was broken. Tina and Roger's story is a prime example.

When Tina pulled into the driveway an hour earlier than normal, she was surprised to see her husband's car in the garage. Roger usually didn't get home from work before 6:00 P.M. What Tina didn't know was that Roger had been coming home well before 6:00 P.M. for several weeks. He had been keeping a dark secret from his wife for months, and he couldn't figure out how to break the news to her. When she pulled into the driveway early that night, he knew it was time to come clean with her.

Tina found Roger sitting in the family room. "You're home early," she said.

"There's something I need to talk with you about, Tina," Roger said glumly.

Tina's first thought was that something had happened to her mother, who was in poor health. "What, Roger?" she said, sitting down next to him. "Is Mom all right?"

"Yes, your mom is fine. That's not the problem. *I'm* the problem."

"What do you mean?"

Roger sighed deeply. "For several weeks now I've been living a lie, Tina."

"A lie? What lie?"

"I . . . I lost my job."

Roger's statement caught Tina completely off guard. "What? When did this happen?"

"Almost two months ago. I was fired."

"Two months ago!" Tina exclaimed, feeling panic. "Every day you get up and say you're going to work. Where have you been going?"

"Some days I look for work. Other days I go downtown and walk around or come back home after you leave. I was wrong to lie to you, I know that. I just couldn't bring myself to tell you. I don't know what else to say other than I really blew it."

Tina dropped her head and sat in silence for a moment. Then her head snapped up quickly. "What about the bills? Have they been paid?"

Roger nodded slowly. "Yes, the bills have all been paid. That's another part of what I have to tell you." Roger paused. His lower lip began to tremble. "I took out a second mortgage on the house and got $25,000. Most of the bills are paid up, but that money is now . . . gone."

"Gone?" Tina said in shocked disbelief. "Twenty-five thousand dollars gone? Where? On what?"

"I don't even know where it all went, Tina, I just spent it," Roger said, beginning to weep. "I'm so sorry." Roger's tears were not only the product of his heavy heart but also a sign that the healing process in their marriage had begun.

Tina was so stunned and angry she could hardly think. She

knew Roger needed her love and forgiveness, but he had lied to her for two long months. How could she ever trust him again?

Roger and Tina talked well into the night and were able to make significant progress toward forgiveness. Despite her hurt and anger over Roger's failure, Tina was committed to him. Roger had been more transparent with her than ever before, and she began to understand the pain of his secret struggle. And Roger understood more than ever just how much his deceit had hurt his wife.

After months of communication and working through their conflict, Tina was able to forgive Roger. But both of them knew the act of forgiveness had not closed the loop. Too much had happened; he had hurt her too deeply. He had perpetuated a devastating lie for two months. Would he do it again? Something had to change for Roger to regain Tina's trust and for their relationship to be fully restored.

The final phase of closing the loop is to rebuild your trust. (See diagram in figure 13.) In minor conflicts, this stage is unnecessary or very easy. When little or no trust is eroded, repairs are mini-

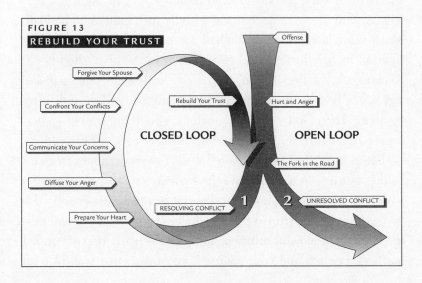

FIGURE 13
REBUILD YOUR TRUST

Forgive Your Spouse
Confront Your Conflicts
Communicate Your Concerns
Diffuse Your Anger
Prepare Your Heart

Rebuild Your Trust

Offense
Hurt and Anger

CLOSED LOOP

OPEN LOOP

The Fork in the Road

RESOLVING CONFLICT   1   2   UNRESOLVED CONFLICT

mal. But for deeper wounds of the heart—like those Tina and Roger, Wayne and Samantha, and Katy and Walker suffered—the need for rebuilding trust is substantial.

When you hurt your spouse deeply, he or she may be willing to grant forgiveness. But this doesn't mean your relationship is completely healed, that you can pick up where you left off and go on as if nothing happened. For true restoration to occur, you must be willing to work to rebuild your spouse's trust over a period of time.

In the book of Nehemiah, Gary and I see a biblical pattern for rebuilding trust in a marriage relationship. Gary will relate the steps that we have gleaned from Nehemiah's experience.

REBUILDING THE WALLS OF YOUR MARRIAGE

Almost 2,400 years ago, the city of Jerusalem lay in ruins. King Nebuchadnezzar of Babylon had ordered his army to plunder and destroy it, tearing down its protective wall and then deporting and enslaving the Jews who lived there (see 2 Chronicles 36:15-21). Among those deported was a godly man named Nehemiah. Many years later, after Persia had conquered Babylon and taken over all its territories, God gave Nehemiah favor in the eyes of Artaxerxes, the Persian king. Artaxerxes allowed Nehemiah and a group of Jews to move back to their homeland and the city of Jerusalem. Then God used Nehemiah to rebuild the wall of Jerusalem so the returning Jews could live in safety and security.

Cities in biblical times needed walls to protect them from invading armies. In a similar way, a marriage relationship needs a wall of protection around it to keep it healthy and secure. This wall is built by faith in God and by developing disciplines and habits that strengthen commitment and trust. When a loop of conflict has been opened and your spouse is wounded, that wall of trust around you begins to crumble. Repeated offenses break down that wall just like the battering rams of an invading army. Hearts are plundered, security is undermined, and trust is eroded.

As Roger and Tina learned, the wall of trust must be rebuilt. The process Nehemiah followed to rebuild the wall of Jerusalem is a good pattern for rebuilding trust in your marriage. Barb and I have identified nine steps in this process.

Step 1: Weep and Seek God

While still in Persia, Nehemiah, the king's cupbearer, heard the troubling news: "Things are not going well for those who returned to the province of Judah. They are in great trouble and disgrace. The wall of Jerusalem has been torn down, and the gates have been burned" (Nehemiah 1:3). What should he do? Ask for a meeting with King Artaxerxes? Gather some people together and head for Jerusalem to do the work? There's nothing wrong with these steps, but that's not what Nehemiah did first. Upon hearing the news, Nehemiah says, "I sat down and wept. In fact, for days I mourned, fasted, and prayed to the God of heaven" (Nehemiah 1:4).

The first step to rebuilding trust in your marriage is to mourn what you have lost and go to God for help. This is how Roger responded. He cried tears of anguish over his sin and tears of relief at uncovering his painful secret. "Tina, I want to change," he said. "I need to change, and I need you. I want to work on our marriage. I know I can't ask you to trust me. But I'm asking for the chance to regain your trust. Will you pray with me about this?"

Step 2: Pray

Next, Nehemiah confessed his own sins and asked God to give him favor with Artaxerxes (see Nehemiah 1:5-11). As Nehemiah prayed, he knew in his heart that he could help to restore the wall around Jerusalem.

How do we respond when the wall is tumbling down around us at home? Some of us cower in fear. Others deny that there is a problem and even try to anesthetize ourselves with alcohol, other drugs, spending, pornography, or anything that feeds our rationalization. Still others get angry. But look at what Nehemiah did. After expressing the pain of his heart, he prayed. And it wasn't just a quick, catchall type of prayer. The second chapter of Nehemiah reveals that he prayed earnestly for four months before he set out to do anything.

The apostle James writes, "The earnest prayer of a righteous person has great power and wonderful results" (James 5:16). When you face the task of rebuilding the wall of trust in your marriage, you need to pray earnestly for God's will to be done. Then you need to trust him as he works out his will in your individual lives and your marriage.

As Roger sat with Tina that night, he prayed, "God, I have wounded Tina deeply and have sinned against her and you. I'm so sorry. Please forgive me. Please give Tina the grace to forgive me as well. I know it will take time, perhaps lots of time. Give me the strength to rebuild her trust in me. If it's your will, and I believe it is, work through us to restore this broken relationship."

Step 3: Communicate Needs Honestly

One day, King Artaxerxes noticed that Nehemiah was not himself. The king said, "Why are you so sad? You aren't sick, are you? You look like a man with deep troubles" (Nehemiah 2:2). God had opened an opportunity for Nehemiah to explain his feelings about the destruction in his homeland, so he told Artaxerxes the sad story.

When the king asked Nehemiah what he wanted to do, Nehemiah didn't just spit out his request. He prayed first, and then asked for the opportunity to go to Jerusalem to rebuild the wall. The king asked how much time he needed. Nehemiah not only gave him a time frame for completing the task but also asked the king for some materials for the rebuilding project. Artaxerxes gave Nehemiah everything he asked for.

Why did this powerful king grant Nehemiah's request? Nehemiah explains, "The king granted these requests, because the gracious hand of God was on me" (Nehemiah 2:8). The rebuilding process works when God is at the center.

In addition to praying for God's guidance for restoring his marriage, Roger had to make his needs known to Tina. Having requested her forgiveness, he also communicated his need for her help in rebuilding the relationship and holding him accountable not to lie anymore. Openness about your hurts and needs is a prerequisite for rebuilding trust.

Step 4: Commit to the Journey

As Nehemiah set off on a journey of hundreds of miles, what went through his mind? He probably had little idea of the extent of the devastation he would encounter. He likely knew even less about the amount of resistance he would face and the hard work needed to rebuild the wall. As the days of travel wore on, he must have battled through a number of doubts about what he had set out to do. But he still went for it. He was committed to do what needed to be done.

The same God who led Nehemiah on his mission is willing to help you and your spouse rebuild your relationship. Are you willing to step out and trust God despite your fears and doubts? You might want to pray something like this: "God, I commit to work on restoring this relationship with my spouse no matter how hard it is or how long it takes. But I need you to go before me. I'm not going unless you lead the way."

When you and your spouse commit to the journey, you remind each other that the relationship is nonnegotiable. You honor the covenant expressed in your marriage vows. You commit to divorce-proof your marriage both for your own sake and for the sake of future generations.

Step 5: Evaluate the Damage

Arriving in Jerusalem, Nehemiah set out to survey the damage done to the wall. The rubble was so great that he couldn't even ride his horse through it. He must have been overwhelmed.

In order to close the loop and rebuild trust, you need to evaluate the damage in your relationship. Admit your failures, acknowledge your offenses, talk about your hurts. Lay it all out there. You can't effectively rebuild and heal if you don't bring all the hurt and anger into the open.

Roger and Tina took time to assess the extent of damage Roger's lie had caused in their relationship. Tina said, "Roger, I don't know how to respond to you. You have kept things from me before, but this is the worst ever. You purposely hid from me that you got fired, got a second mortgage, and spent all the money. I don't know which makes me feel most betrayed. They all make me angry. How am I ever going to trust you again?"

"You're right, Tina," Roger replied. "I haven't been honest with you. But I knew I had to tell you the truth. It was eating me up inside. By telling you, I feel better, but you feel worse. I hurt you either way, didn't I?"

"Yes, but I need to know the truth."

As they continued to pick through the rubble, they acknowledged that Roger still had no job. Furthermore, his self-confidence was at an all-time low, making it difficult for him to believe he could ever find a good job, much less build a successful career. His frivolous and uncontrolled spending had placed their finances in serious jeopardy. They were in danger of losing everything they had.

Worst of all, Roger had formed a habit of deceit he didn't know how to break. He felt powerless to change his life. And

Tina felt hurt, betrayed, and angry. She loved her husband, but she wondered if he would ever change.

Step 6: Formulate a Plan

As the drama unfolded in Jerusalem, Nehemiah went to the people: "'You know full well the tragedy of our city. It lies in ruins, and its gates are burned. Let us rebuild the wall of Jerusalem and rid ourselves of this disgrace!' Then I told them about how the gracious hand of God had been on me, and about my conversation with the king. They replied at once, 'Good! Let's rebuild the wall!' So they began the good work" (Nehemiah 2:17-18).

In his challenge, Nehemiah urged the people to get started on the project. He reminded them to trust God to help them get the job done. And he not only came with the blessing of the king and some materials but also had a plan for completing the work. Part of that plan directed the people to rebuild the portion of the wall that was in front of their own homes. What better motivation could Nehemiah have provided?

Trusting God and devising a plan are critical to the process of rebuilding trust. You may feel helpless to change your situation or behavior in your own power. Perhaps you have tried and failed repeatedly. You need to devise a solid plan while trusting God to make it possible.

When Roger confessed to Tina, he knew he had caused great pain to her and great damage to their relationship. He was willing to rebuild the relationship, but he wanted her to be willing to try as well. Here's how he approached the challenge.

"Tina, I know I have lost your trust through what I did. But I also know we can rebuild trust together. Other couples have done it, and we can too. I realize I can't change on my own. I need to make my relationship with God a priority and let him work in my life. I know it will take time, but I also know God can do anything.

"I want us to work out a specific plan for what we can do. I'm willing to get the counseling I need, to rebuild my career, and to learn how to handle finances correctly. We probably need to see a counselor together as well.

"Please work with me, and let's restore our marriage."

A lot of people in Tina's situation would just throw in the towel rather than try to put their marriages back together again. They have little hope that such huge problems can be solved, and they are unwilling to put in the time and effort to rebuild the relationship. But just as the people in Jerusalem declared, "Let us start rebuilding," so Barb and I have seen many people like Tina respond to their spouses by saying, "Yes, we can do it. Let's work out a plan and start rebuilding. It won't be easy, but we can do it."

Step 7: Begin the Work

Chapters 3 and 4 of Nehemiah describe the actual rebuilding of the wall. Nehemiah wrote, "At last the wall was completed to half its original height around the entire city, for the people had worked very hard" (Nehemiah 4:6). Sounds like good, old-fashioned perseverance. When you are rebuilding a broken relationship, do you throw yourself into it wholeheartedly?

There is a honeymoon effect in the process of rebuilding marital trust. A couple launches into it with a lot of hope and energy, the healing begins, and they think, *Hey, this isn't so hard!* But they often fail to realize how much time and hard work it takes to complete the rebuilding. Soon the enthusiasm wanes, and they often slide back into their old habit patterns.

One big difference between Nehemiah's rebuilding project and our attempts at rebuilding trust is the amount of time involved. While the Jerusalem wall was rebuilt in a miraculous fifty-two days, it may take much longer to rebuild a relationship.

The element of time can work in your favor in at least two

ways. First, it takes time to heal the pain—often months or years. We often tell people at our conferences or callers on our radio show that when there is a serious breach of trust in the marriage, such as adultery, it often takes eighteen to twenty-four months to rebuild the trust. But as the weeks and months go by, you should experience greater levels of healing.

Second, you need time to inject some positive experiences into a relationship that is accustomed to pain. As you spend time nurturing the relationship and storing up positive memories, the healing process is encouraged. You also need time to seek biblical counseling from a professional counselor or pastor who is gifted in counseling. Often a mentoring couple, mature in their relationship with Christ, can be a great asset in the healing process.

Roger followed through on receiving biblical counseling. He committed himself to the process and began to see great results. Through counseling he realized his great fear of not measuring up to his own expectations, which prompted him to develop a pattern of covering up his failures. He took great strides in learning to communicate honestly with Tina, even about his shortcomings.

Tina stuck with him during this tough time, which encouraged Roger to develop deeper trust in her. This allowed him to risk greater emotional intimacy with her, sharing more of his thoughts, feelings, and fears. And the more he opened up to Tina, the more she was able to trust him. They were on the road to healing.

Another element that contributes to the honeymoon effect in rebuilding trust is the cost involved. You may go into the process assuming all you need to invest is time. But it may end up costing you much more. Look what it cost Tina and Roger. It cost them their pride. They faced many months working their way out of the financial hole Roger had dug for them. The process taxed their sense of security as they took risks to open their hearts to each other. As you get to work on rebuilding trust, be ready to pay the price.

Step 8: Trust God through the Inevitable Resistance

Nehemiah faced resistance continually throughout his project in Jerusalem. He had many enemies who did not want to see the wall rebuilt. They tried to stir up the people against him, planting doubts in their minds. They conspired to harm him. They accused him of scheming to become a king and lead the Jews in revolt. They even hired a prophet to try to intimidate him. In each case, Nehemiah prayed to God for guidance and asked him to lead the way. This prayer is typical: "Hear us, O our God, for we are being mocked. May their scoffing fall back on their own heads, and may they themselves become captives in a foreign land!" (Nehemiah 4:4).

Satan is threatened when you and your spouse grow in trust and intimacy. He is actively at work trying to keep you isolated from each other, trying to keep you suspicious, and distrustful. So when you set out to rebuild trust in your marriage, be aware that the enemy will be there to discourage and deter you. For example, just when you are making good progress, someone may come along and say something like, "It will never work for you two. It's good that you have forgiven your spouse, but you will never be able to trust him again." It is especially difficult when such comments come from family members or close friends.

But God is eager for you to close the loops in your marriage by experiencing forgiveness and restoration. He will empower you to work through the resistance and discouragement. And as you allow God's Spirit to guide you, you will succeed. The apostle John said, "The Spirit who lives in you is greater than the spirit who lives in the world" (1 John 4:4).

Roger and Tina experienced resistance as they began to rebuild their relationship. Tina continually battled an internal voice that said, "You're not going to trust him again, are you? If you do, you're nuts! He'll never change."

Tina's parents had already given up on Roger. "He's too far gone," her father had said. "Your mother and I would never have treated each other that way. Kick him out. He's a disgrace to our family."

One of Tina's good friends, who was recently divorced, also had her doubts. "I know exactly what you're going through, Tina," she said. "But I don't understand why you think Roger can ever change. He's a chronic liar. My ex told me again and again that he would stop drinking, and it only got worse."

Messages like these can sow seeds of profound doubt. The Jews in Nehemiah's day experienced plenty of doubt: "Then the people of Judah began to complain that the workers were becoming tired. There was so much rubble to be moved that we could never get it done by ourselves" (Nehemiah 4:10). They were wearing down under attacks from every angle.

Then Nehemiah had the people do an amazing thing: "From then on, only half my men worked while the other half stood guard with spears, shields, bows, and coats of mail. The officers stationed themselves behind the people of Judah who were building the wall. The common laborers carried on their work with one hand supporting their load and one hand holding a weapon. All the builders had a sword belted to their side. The trumpeter stayed with me to sound the alarm" (Nehemiah 4:16-18).

What an incredible response! No throwing in the towel for this wall-builder. He instructed the people to work with one hand and to defend themselves with the other.

This passage of the Bible is so relevant to us today. When you are restoring your marriage relationship, you need to work hard and persevere when times get tough. You need to confront your doubts, realize they are not from God, and pray, pray, pray. At the same time, you need to be on the alert to defend your marriage from future attacks. Never let down your guard. Stand against anything and everything that threatens to tear down what you are building up. (If you need additional help, see our book *Guard Your Heart*.)

Step 9: Work toward Completion

At one point Nehemiah was able to write, "So on October 2 the wall was finally finished—just fifty-two days after we had begun. When our enemies and the surrounding nations heard about it, they were frightened and humiliated. They realized that this work had been done with the help of our God" (Nehemiah 6:15-16). Can you imagine Nehemiah's joy at writing, "The wall was finally finished"? What a sense of accomplishment. In reality, the major part of the work was done. But, as some scholars suggest, the Jews continued to patch the wall for some time.

Rebuilding trust and restoring marital intimacy after offenses is a job that is never fully completed. Each area of healing continues to need maintenance long after you have closed the loop. But that doesn't mean you shouldn't keep moving in the direction of completion and closure in the process. Enjoy each victory along the way, but continue to allow God to do his "finish work" in your marriage.

As you do, something wonderful happens. Your marriage will be a strong testimony of the power and grace of God. Just like Nehemiah's detractors, those who didn't see any hope for you will have to say, "Wow, look what God accomplished in their lives!" That's your great hope, even in the middle of the work. You are not alone in the rebuilding process. God is at the center of the work. It is his desire to restore your relationship and divorce-proof your marriage. He is the God of restoration and reconciliation. He is the God of closing loops.

YOU CAN DO IT!

The next conflict you face will inevitably be accompanied by a few doubts: Can I really do this? Can I successfully apply the principles for resolving conflict and healing hurts I've learned? Or will it be "same old same old" when it comes to trying to close the loop?

Yes, you *can* do it! Barb and I say that with confidence because God is on your side when you set out to heal the hurts in your marriage. Consider the New Testament's encouragement to Christians:

> Therefore, since we have been made right in God's sight by faith, we have peace with God because of what Jesus Christ our Lord has done for us. Because of our faith, Christ has brought us into this place of highest privilege where we now stand, and we confidently and joyfully look forward to sharing God's glory.
>
> We can rejoice, too, when we run into problems and trials, for we know that they are good for us—they help us learn to endure. And endurance develops strength of character in us, and character strengthens our confident expectation of salvation. And this expectation will not disappoint us. For we know how dearly God loves us, because he has given us the Holy Spirit to fill our hearts with his love. (Romans 5:1-5)

Notice the solid platform God provides for closing the loop. You have been made right in God's sight by your faith in Christ. As a result, you enjoy peace with God. No matter how painful the conflict, no matter how difficult the healing process, God has you in the hollow of his hand and he's not going to let you go.

As a result, you can actually rejoice in the midst of your struggle with hurt. Why? Because God will get you through it. Jesus—

not your intellect, your bank account, or even your marriage counselor—is your basis for hope.

As you rejoice, you will build endurance as a couple. You will develop a lifestyle of hanging in there even when you don't know how you're going to get out of a seemingly intolerable situation. Endurance is the fine art of keeping your head down in a blinding snowstorm and pushing forward. Sometimes it seems that the blizzard of conflict will never let up, but it will. You just need to stay obedient and maintain God's course until the storm quiets.

As you hang in there, you will develop strong character. Character isn't built while you're lying on the beach sipping lemonade with everything coming up roses. Rather, character in marriage is shaped as you work your way through conflicts and resolve to face all obstacles and temptations and not give up.

And where does character lead? To confident expectation—hope. As you and your spouse trust God to help you close loops and heal hurts, you'll be able to say, "Our marriage isn't just getting by, we're beginning to soar. We have a good marriage that is growing into a great marriage. Our kids don't ever have to worry that their parents will get a divorce. We are growing closer every day."

The loop of conflict you are facing can be closed. Take the first step today. It is possible. It works. You can do it! Go for it!

CAMPAIGN RESOURCES FOR DIVORCE-PROOFING AMERICA'S MARRIAGES

*D*ear friends,

The resources for the Divorce-Proofing America's Marriages campaign are designed *for you*—to help you divorce-proof your marriage. You and your spouse can certainly read and study these books as a couple. But it's only when you meet with a small group that is committed to divorce-proofing their marriages as well that you'll fully experience the power of these ideas. There's power when believers unite in a common cause. There's power when men and women keep each other accountable. To take on this challenge, you must have a group of friends who are encouraging you every step of the way.

There are several ways you can connect to a small group:

* Start your own Divorce-Proofing America's Marriages small group in your church or neighborhood. For workbooks, leader's guides, videos, and other resources for your small group, call 888-ROSBERG (888-767-2374) or visit our Web site at **www.divorceproof.com**.

✸ Give this information to your pastor or elders at your local church. They may want to host a Divorce-Proofing America's Marriages small group in your church.

✸ Call America's Family Coaches at 888-ROSBERG (888-767-2374), or e-mail us at **afc@afclive.com** and we will connect you with people and churches who are interested in Divorce-Proofing America's Marriages.

Yes, together we can launch a nationwide campaign and see countless homes transformed into covenant homes. But beware. If we do not teach these principles to our own children, we risk missing the greatest opportunity of all: to pass our legacy of godly homes to the next generation. Barb and I believe that, *for the sake of the next generation,* there is no more worthy cause. This holy fire must purify our own homes first.

Gary and Barb Rosberg

DIVORCE-PROOF YOUR MARRIAGE
ISBN 0-8423-4995-2
Audio CD (3 CDs) ISBN 0-8423-6592-3
Audiocassette (2 cassettes) ISBN 0-8423-6894-9

DISCOVER THE LOVE OF YOUR LIFE ALL OVER AGAIN (workbook)
ISBN 0-8423-7342-X

2003 GOLD MEDALLION WINNER

Your house is weatherproofed. But is your marriage divorce-proofed? In this foundational book of the Divorce-Proofing America's Marriages campaign, Gary and Barb show couples how to keep their marriages safe from the threat of divorce. Divorce doesn't happen suddenly. Over months and years couples can slide from the dream to disappointment and eventually to emotional divorce. However, they can stop the slide by learning to love in six unique ways. Small groups will enjoy the *Discover the Love of Your Life All Over Again* workbook, which includes eight sessions. Together couples will practice healing hurt in their marriages, meeting spouses' needs, strengthening each other through difficult times, guarding their marriage against threats, celebrating their spouses, and renewing their love for each other daily. A weekly devotion and assignment will help couples practice what they learn with the encouragement of couples who are committed to the same goal of divorce-proofing their marriages. This workbook includes an easy-to-follow leader's guide.

THE 5 LOVE NEEDS OF MEN AND WOMEN
ISBN 0-8423-4239-7
Audiocassette (2 cassettes) ISBN 0-8423-3587-0

SERVING LOVE (workbook)
ISBN 0-8423-7343-8

You, too, can learn how to become your spouse's best friend with *The Five Love Needs of Men and Women* book and workbook. In this book, Gary talks to women about the deepest needs of their husbands, and Barb talks to men about the most intimate needs of their wives. You'll discover the deep yearnings of your spouse. And when you join a group studying the *Serving Love* workbook, you will learn how to understand and meet your spouse's needs within a circle of encouraging friends. They can help you find ways to meet those needs day after day, week after week. The workbook includes eight group sessions, three weekly activities, and ideas for a date night with your spouse. Easy-to-follow leader's guide included.

GUARD YOUR HEART
ISBN 0-8423-5732-7

GUARDING LOVE (workbook)
ISBN 0-8423-7344-6

We all need to guard our hearts and marriages. It's only in a couples small group, among like-minded friends, that you can get the solid support you need to withstand attacks on your marriage. In *Guard Your Heart,* Gary and Barb Rosberg outline the unique dangers and temptations husbands and wives face. In the *Guarding Love* workbook, the Rosbergs give you the tools to show your small group how to hold each other accountable to guarding their marriages—no matter the cost.

Do you know of a marriage in your church or neighborhood that is vulnerable to attack? Start a small group for that couple with the *Guarding Love* workbook as a resource. Or invite that couple to a small group that is reading and applying this book and workbook. The workbook includes eight exciting group sessions and an easy-to-follow leader's guide.

HEALING THE HURT IN YOUR MARRIAGE:
BEYOND CONFLICT TO FORGIVENESS
ISBN 1-58997-104-3

In *Healing the Hurt in Your Marriage: Beyond Conflict to Forgiveness,* Gary and Barb Rosberg show you how to forgive past hurt in your marriage and close the loop on unresolved conflict.

Restore an honest, whole relationship with your spouse. You probably know a dozen marriages that are deteriorating because one spouse is holding a grudge or because the husband and wife have never resolved their conflict, hurt, or anger. And most marriages have past hurts that are hindering the ongoing relationship. Gary and Barb show you how to break free of these past hurts and experience wholeness again. The most effective way to heal wounds is within the circle of encouraging believers who understand, know, and sympathize with you in the common struggles in marriage.

RENEWING YOUR LOVE: DEVOTIONS FOR COUPLES
ISBN 0-8423-7346-2

Have the demands of everyday life pressed in on your marriage? Has your to-do list become more important than your relationship with your spouse? Is the TV the center of your home or the love you and your spouse share? This devotional from America's Family Coaches, Gary and Barb Rosberg, will help you and your spouse focus on your marriage, your relationship, and the love of your life. Let Gary and Barb guide you through thirty days of renewal and recommitment to your marriage by reviewing forgiving love, serving love, persevering love, guarding love, celebrating love, and renewing love through the lens of Scripture, reflection, prayer, and application.

Look for a persevering love book in the future from Gary and Barbara Rosberg and Tyndale House Publishers. This book will help you weather the storms of life without losing the passion for your spouse.

Also watch for a celebrating love book from your favorite family coaches, Gary and Barb Rosberg. This book will give you creative ideas on how to keep the fire and passion alive in your marriage.

Become a marriage champion and divorce-proof your home, your church, and your community today

Contact your local bookstore that sells Christian books for all of the resources of the Divorce-Proofing America's Marriages campaign
or
call 888-ROSBERG (888-767-2374)
or
visit our ministry Web site at www.afclive.com

or visit our campaign Web site at www.divorceproof.com

40 UNFORGETTABLE DATES WITH YOUR MATE
ISBN 0-8423-6106-5

When's the last time you and your spouse went on an unforgettable date? Saying "I do" certainly doesn't mean you're finished working at your marriage. Nobody ever put a tank of gas in a car and expected it to run for years. But lots of couples are running on emotional fumes of long-ago dates. Truth is, if you're not dating your spouse, your relationship is not growing. Bring the zing back into your marriage with *40 Unforgettable Dates with Your Mate,* a book that gives husbands and wives ideas on how they can meet the five love needs of their spouse. Wives, get the inside scoop on your husband. Men, discover what your wife finds irresistible. Gary and Barb Rosberg show you how, step-by-step, in fun and creative dates.

CONNECTING WITH YOUR WIFE
ISBN 0-8423-6020-4

Want to understand your wife better? Barbara Rosberg talks directly to men about what makes women tick. She'll help you understand your wife's emotional wiring as she shows you how to communicate more effectively and connect sexually in a way that's more satisfying to your spouse. She also reveals the single best thing you can do for your marriage—and why it's so important.

NOTES

CHAPTER ONE: Have You Ever Been Hurt?

1. Diane Sollee, "What's the Number One Predictor of Divorce?" <www. smartmarriages.com>.
2. Neil Clark Warren, *Date . . . Or Soul Mate?* (Nashville: Nelson, 2002), 176.

CHAPTER TWO: Blindsided by an Offense

1. Michele Weiner-Davis, *The Divorce Remedy: The Proven 7-Step Program for Saving Your Marriage* (New York: Simon & Schuster, 2001), 39.
2. James Dobson, *Straight Talk* (Dallas: Word, 1991), 183.
3. Gary Smalley with John Trent, *Love Is a Decision* (Dallas: Word, 1989), 146.

CHAPTER FOUR: Where Did You Learn to Resolve Conflict?

1. Kim France, "Sleeping with the Enemy," *Mademoiselle* (October 1991): 146.
2. Sue Bowders, "Salvaging the Troubled Relationship: When It's Up to You," *Cosmopolitan* (September 1991): 146.
3. Peter Gerstenzang, "Good Ways to Say Bad Things," *Cosmopolitan* (December 1991): 90.
4. Robert Lewis and William Hendricks, *Rocking the Roles: Building a Win-Win Marriage* (Colorado Springs, Colo.: NavPress, 1991), 68.

CHAPTER SIX: Red Lights on the Road to Healing

1. C. S. Lewis, *Mere Christianity* (New York: Macmillan, 1952), 114.
2. Sandra D. Wilson, *Released from Shame: Recovery for Adult Children of Dysfunctional Families* (Downers Grove, Ill.: InterVarsity, 1990), 10.

CHAPTER SEVEN: Nonnegotiables for Closing the Loop

1. C. S. Lewis, *The Problem of Pain* (New York: Macmillan, 1962), 93.
2. Linda J. Waite and Maggie Gallagher, *The Case for Marriage: Why Married People Are Happier, Healthier, and Better Off Financially* (New York: Doubleday, 2000), 75.

CHAPTER EIGHT: Prepare Your Heart

1. Quoted in Tim Kimmel, *Little House on the Freeway: Help for the Hurried Home* (Portland, Ore.: Multnomah, 1987), 31.
2. Bill and Lynne Hybels, *Fit to Be Tied: Making Marriage Last a Lifetime* (Grand Rapids, Mich.: Zondervan, 1991), 178.
3. Ibid.
4. Lisa Beamer and Ken Abraham, *Let's Roll!: Ordinary People, Extraordinary Courage* (Wheaton, Ill.: Tyndale House, 2002), 105–106.
5. Ibid, 106.

CHAPTER TEN: Communicate Your Concerns

1. Gary Smalley and John Trent, *Love Is a Decision: Ten Proven Principles to Energize Your Marriage and Family* (Dallas: Word, 1989), 44.

CHAPTER ELEVEN: Confront Your Conflicts

1. John Gottman, Ph.D. and Nan Silver, *The Seven Principles for Making Marriage Work* (New York: Three Rivers Press, 1999), 2; 27–34.

CHAPTER TWELVE: Forgive Your Spouse

1. Lewis B. Smedes, *Forgive and Forget: Healing the Hurts We Don't Deserve (San Francisco: Harper & Row, 1984), 133.
2. F. F. Bruce quoted in Jerry Bridges, *Transforming Grace: Living Confidently in God's Unfailing Love* (Colorado Springs, Colo.: NavPress, 1991), 205.
3. Lewis B. Smedes, *Forgive and Forget*, 39.
4. David Stoop and James Masteller, *Forgiving Our Parents, Forgiving Ourselves: Healing Adult Children of Dysfunctional Families* (Ann Arbor, Mich.: Vine Books, 1991), 263.

ABOUT THE AUTHORS

*D*r. **Gary and Barbara Rosberg** are America's Family Coaches—equipping and encouraging America's families to live and finish life well. Having been married for nearly thirty years, Gary and Barbara have a unique message for couples. The Rosbergs have committed the next decade of their ministry to divorce-proofing America's marriages. *Divorce-Proof Your Marriage,* campaign cornerstone book and 2003 Gold Medallion winner, equips couples to strengthen their marriage to avoid the slide toward disconnection and emotional divorce.

Other books the Rosbergs have written together include *Discover the Love of Your Life All Over Again* (workbook companion to *Divorce-Proof Your Marriage*), the best-selling *The Five Love Needs of Men and Women* (with companion workbook, *Serving Love*), *Guard Your Heart* (with companion workbook, *Guarding Love*), *Renewing Your Love: Devotions for Couples,* and *40 Unforgettable Dates with Your Mate.*

Together Gary and Barbara host a nationally syndicated, daily radio program, *America's Family Coaches . . . LIVE!* On this live call-in program heard in cities all across the country, they coach callers on many family-related issues. The Rosbergs also host a Saturday radio program heard in the Midwest on the award-winning secular WHO Radio.

Their flagship conference, "Discover the Love of Your

Life . . . *All Over Again"* is bringing the Divorce-Proofing America's Marriages Campaign to cities across America. They are on the national speaking teams for FamilyLife's "A Weekend to Remember" conferences and "Rekindling the Romance" arena events for couples. Gary also has spoken to thousands of men at Promise Keepers stadium events annually since 1996 and to parents and adolescents at Focus on the Family "Life on the Edge Tour" events.

Gary, who earned his Ed.D. from Drake University, has been a marriage and family counselor for twenty years. He founded and coaches CrossTrainers, a fifteen-year men's Bible study and accountability group of more than five hundred men.

Barbara, who earned a B.F.A. from Drake University, has written *Connecting with Your Wife* in addition to several other books with Gary. She also speaks to women, coaching and encouraging them by emphasizing their incredible value and worth.

The Rosbergs live outside Des Moines, Iowa, and are the parents of two adult daughters: Sarah, who lives outside Des Moines with her husband, Scott, and their two sons; and Missy, who lives in Branson, Missouri, with her husband, Cooper.

For more information on the ministries of
America's Family Coaches, contact:

America's Family Coaches
2540 106th Street, Suite 101
Des Moines, Iowa 50322
1-888-ROSBERG
Ministry Web site—www.afclive.com

Campaign Web site—www.divorceproof.com

Tune In to
America's Family Coaches
. . . LIVE!

Listen every weekday for strong coaching on all your marriage, family, and relationship questions. On this interactive, call-in broadcast, Gary and Barbara Rosberg tackle real-life issues by coaching callers on many of today's hottest topics. Tune in and be encouraged by America's leading family coaches.

For a listing of radio stations broadcasting
America's Family Coaches . . . LIVE!
call 1-888-ROSBERG
or
visit our Web site at www.afclive.com.

FOCUS ON THE FAMILY®

Welcome to the *Family!*

Whether you received this book as a gift, borrowed it, or purchased it yourself, we're glad you read it. It's just one of the many helpful, insightful, and encouraging resources produced by Focus on the Family.

In fact, that's what Focus on the Family is all about—providing inspiration, information, and biblically based advice to people in all stages of life.

It began in 1977 with the vision of one man, Dr. James Dobson, a licensed psychologist and author of 18 best-selling books on marriage, parenting, and family. Alarmed by the societal, political, and economic pressures that were threatening the existence of the American family, Dr. Dobson founded Focus on the Family with one employee and a once-a-week radio broadcast aired on only 36 stations.

Now an international organization, the ministry is dedicated to preserving Judeo-Christian values and strengthening and encouraging families through the life-changing message of Jesus Christ. Focus ministries reach families worldwide through 10 separate radio broadcasts, two television news features, 13 publications, 18 Web sites, and a steady series of books and award-winning films and videos for people of all ages and interests.

• • •

For more information about the ministry, or if we can be of help to your family, simply write to Focus on the Family, Colorado Springs, CO 80995 or call (800) A-FAMILY (232-6459). Friends in Canada may write Focus on the Family, PO Box 9800, Stn Terminal, Vancouver, BC V6B 4G3 or call (800) 661-9800. Visit our Web site—www.family.org—to learn more about Focus on the Family or to find out if there is an associate office in your country.

We'd love to hear from you!